Augustus John Cuthbert Hare

A winter at Mentone

Augustus John Cuthbert Hare

A winter at Mentone

ISBN/EAN: 9783337257989

Printed in Europe, USA, Canada, Australia, Japan

Cover: Foto ©Andreas Hilbeck / pixelio.de

More available books at **www.hansebooks.com**

A
Winter at ~~~~

"If you would have ~~~~ and, in a short time to ~~~~ with him some card or book describing ~~~~ country wherein he travelleth, which will be a good key to his enquiry."—*Lord Bacon.*

LONDON:
WERTHEIM, MACINTOSH, & HUNT,
24, PATERNOSTER ROW,
AND 23, HOLLES STREET, CAVENDISH SQUARE.

TO

MY FELLOW SOJOURNERS

IN

BEAUTIFUL MENTONE;

THESE PAGES

ARE

DEDICATED IN GRATEFUL REMEMBRANCE

OF THE

MANY HAPPY HOURS

PASSED IN THEIR SOCIETY.

PREFACE.

The non-existence of any Guide-book to Mentone, or of any history of Monaco and its neighbourhood, except the small summary of Monsieur Rendu, has induced the author to publish the following notes, descriptive of five months spent at Mentone, from November, 1860, to May, 1861.

The accounts of the excursions are derived from personal experience. The many local traditions and histories which have been added, are due to the assistance of the Mentonese residents, whose ready kindness and sympathy in any undertaking, cannot fail to impress every stranger who visits them.

The materials for the History of Monaco, have been drawn partly from the admirable pamphlet of Dr. Bottini, on "L'Annexation," and partly from the manuscript collections formed by the late Colonel Trenca, and extracted from the archives at Turin.

INTRODUCTION.

THOSE who merely pass through Mentone in travelling from Nice to Genoa, can form a very faint conception of the beauty and interest which lie hidden around it, and of which the town itself is only a single type. It is in its secluded valleys, or its deep orange-groves, along the banks of its torrents, or amid the heights of the wild mountain-chain which forms its background, that the principal charm of Mentone is to be found. No place combines more of the southern beauty of Sorrento and Amalfi, with the savage grandeur of the Abruzzi, or of the lower ranges of the Swiss Alps. The excursions are endless, so that good walkers, or even riders, who remain there for the whole winter, need scarcely ever retrace their steps, and may yet have a daily expedition, in almost every description of scenery. Much of the neighbourhood is still unexplored by English travellers, and is likely to offer rich sources of interest and curiosity. The desolate rock cities of Peglia and Peglione, have passed entirely unheeded till within the last year, though the former contains remains of domestic gothic architecture, which may be compared, on a small scale, with those of Venice, while the latter rivals the Grecian Meteora, in the strange picturesqueness of its situation. The two neighbouring petty sovereignties, the miniature, but still existing principality of Monaco, and the extinct and ruined Dolceacqua, are interesting, as well from their scenery and the buildings they contain, as from the strange vicissitudes in the history of the two great families of Grimaldi and Doria, which have so long been their rulers. The more distant Taggia, and Ghiandola, with its rugged mountains and rushing stream, though little visited, are equally attractive.

The geological and botanical resources of the great oolitic mountain chain, which bounds the land view from Mentone on every side, form an abundant field for research. Many strange mountain peaks and rock caverns still remain unvisited and unknown. But, above all, the neighbourhood of Mentone will afford employment to the painter, whether he prefers the pines and orange-groves of the sunny shore, the dark sculptured streets and marble balconies of the old Riviera towns, or the wild position of the ruined strongholds, in the heart of the neighbouring mountains.

The language spoken by the lower classes at Mentone is a branch of the Nizzard patois, a harsh, guttural Italian, quite unintelligible to those who are only accustomed to that language in its purity. Since the annexation however, French, which is universally spoken by the upper classes, has begun to creep into ordinary use. The language of the neighbouring villages, varies with every two or three miles, and its origin might form an interesting subject for investigation. At Castellare, a mountain town only three miles from Mentone, many of the words in common use are Spanish, handed down from the time of the Spanish protection at Monaco; and in like manner, in the rock-built citadel of Esa, and in other places which have been Moorish strongholds, words of Arabic still linger, and these may also be found in the names of their surrounding mountains.

The accommodation for visitors at Mentone is rapidly improving, with the increase of foreign winter residents. The town contains several excellent hotels. Of these, the Hotel Vittoria is near the entrance from Nice, the Hotel des Quatre Nations is in the centre of the principal street, and the Hotel Turin is near the Port; the principal rooms in all these look upon the sea. The Hotel de Londres, which is situated at about a quarter-of-a-mile from the town, on the Nice road, is an excellent and well-managed house; all the rooms in this hotel are generally taken én pension for the whole winter, though the position is rather more exposed and colder than that of the other hotels. The Pension Anglaise, of Monsieur Clerici, is a large house, in a sheltered and beautiful situation on the Genoa side of the town; this is much resorted to by the patients of the English physician, Dr. Bennett, who makes it his winter residence. The terms of this pension are about eight francs a-day. An English lady is proposing to open a new pension at a large house on the east of the town, which, from its sheltered and level situation, and its surrounding scenery, is likely to form a most attractive residence for invalids.

Almost all the principal houses in the place are let as lodgings, the original inhabitants either removing to smaller houses for the season, or retiring to the ground-floor or attics, and giving up all their best rooms. Apartments may be secured beforehand by writing to Mr. Willoughby, the English grocer, who is also the general house-agent; he will send a list of the houses which are disengaged, and will engage what is wanted. He is equally useful in recommending servants, as a long residence at Mentone has made him acquainted with the character of most of the natives. The amount of house-rent is much the same at Mentone as at other places in Italy; the first floor of a house, which contains probably two sitting rooms and four or five bed rooms, costing from £60 to £70 for the season, the upper floors being cheaper. Other things are very dear at Mentone. There is a difficulty in procuring good food of any kind, and the charges made by the hotels for sending out dinners are very high for Italy. Good cooks, may, however, be engaged at Nice early in the season, and will make arrangements for obtaining provisions from thence. The meat at Mentone is essentially bad, the sheep being fed on lemons and the scanty herbage on the sea-shore. There is an utter absence of grass or pasture of any kind, and owing to this, all the butter comes from Milan, and when the passage of the Col di Tenda is snowed up in the winter, it often cannot be obtained at all. The charges made for carriages are enormous, and their owners trust to the scarcity of any means of conveyance for exacting the sums they demand; these, however, will necessarily be lowered, as the increase of strangers induces the importation of fresh carriages from Nice. At present, donkeys afford the only means of locomotion within the reach of the poorer visitors; indeed, these are constantly employed for expeditions, as the only roads which can be traversed by carriages, besides the great Riviera road, are that which branches off to Monaco, and the road to Turin, which as yet is only finished as far as Monti, four miles from Mentone.

During the winter we spent at Mentone, we had months of alternate wet and fine weather. In December it rained almost every day, but during the intervals between the showers, owing to the immense power of the sun, the ground became perfectly dry in an hour, and the climate was delightful, one degree of frost being the greatest amount of cold ever felt. January was a month of cloudless sunshine, with a clear and stimulating air, and was, perhaps, the pleasantest part of the whole season, as the weather was not so hot as to make long expeditions disagreeable, and quite warm enough to admit of sitting out the greater part of the day. During February it rained almost constantly, and the weather was hot and relaxing. March, which brings with it the July flowers of England, was fine, with occasional cold winds. In April, the weather was alternately wet and fine. After we left, May was a month of unclouded summer, but not oppressively hot. Throughout the winter we seldom wanted a fire, except on wet days, or in the evening; and in January it was often hot enough to breakfast at nine o'clock, with windows open to the ground.

The difference between the climate of Nice and that of Mentone, is felt at once on passing the Turbith, a mountain 3000 feet high, which is crossed between the two towns; the sharp winds of Nice being scarcely felt at Mentone, which is also free from the clouds of dust, which often render a residence at Nice so disagreeable.

St. Remo possesses a climate almost as mild as that of Mentone, and is a place where new lodging-houses are beginning to attract foreign residents; but, though beautiful and picturesque in itself, it is entirely deficient in the varied excursions and scenery, which make Mentone so attractive, and it has not yet been reached by many of the English comforts, which may now be obtained at Mentone.

The following account of the climate of Mentone and its effects, is taken from an admirable paper by Dr. Henry Bennett, first published in the *Lancet*, July 7, 1860:—

"Owing to a complete protection from the west, north-west, north, and north-east winds, and owing to the reflection of the sun's rays from the sides of the naked mountains, which form an ampitheatre around it, the climate of Mentone is rather warmer than that of Nice—indeed, warmer than that of any part of the northern or central parts of Italy. This fact is proved by the presence of groves of large, healthy lemon trees, which occupy the sheltered ravines and the warmer hill sides, wherever water can be obtained, constant irrigation, summer and winter, being necessary for their cultivation. When the thermometer descended to zero several nights consecutively near the sea-shore, and slight films of ice formed on flagons of water on the road and near the torrents, profound dismay was occasioned in the minds of the natives, whose principal riches are the lemon-groves. For several nights many of them sat up, in the greatest consternation, watching the thermometer. Indeed, there was a complete panic with reference to this lamentable and unheard of condition of the weather. Such feelings and fears plainly indicated that frost and snow were very unusual and unwelcome visitors.

" The foreign population of Mentone numbered about three hundred, and contained representatives of nearly all the European nations. The French and English were, however, the most numerous, each family containing generally one invalid. Most of the latter were suffering from pulmonary consumption. Those who were in the early or even secondary stages of the disease, and had vitality and constitutional stamina left, mostly did well. . . . Those who were in the latter stages of the disease, on the contrary, appeared to derive but little benefit from the change. The disease seemed to progress slowly, but steadily. . . .

" Several patients who always suffered from bronchitis in England were quite free from it at Mentone, owing to the dryness of the atmosphere. . . . . It is easy to understand that a dry, bracing, cool and invigorating climate should have a beneficial influence on the respiratory mucous membrane of the persons who have still some of the vital powers of youth or some constitutional stamina left. When we add to this, all but daily exercise in the open air through the winter, in the midst of magnificent scenery, removal from the cares, anxieties and duties of ordinary life, pleasant social intercourse with fellow sufferers and their families, all tuned to the same unison of cheerful and hopeful resignation, we certainly have united all the hygienic influences calculated to renovate the general health, and to arrest the development of tubercular disease. Indeed, to me it is a question whether a warmer and milder winter climate, which is only to be found in a tropical or sub-tropical region, is not less favourable to the recovery of health under such circumstances, always provided rigid attention be paid to the precautions necessary in a climate where the temperature so constantly varies.

"To derive that benefit, however, from the climate of Mentone, and of the south of Europe generally, which it is capable of affording in pulmonary consumption, the most rigid attention should be paid to the hygienic rules peculiar to these regions during the winter season. It should never be forgotten that in winter the heat is sun-heat, and that the air, barring its influence, is usually cold. Warm clothes and woollen outer garments should be used. In dressing for out of doors, a thermometer, placed *outside a north room*, should always be consulted. The hours for out of door exercise should be between ten and four, and the return should be so arranged as to secure the arrival at home before sunset. The Italian physicians appear to attach a mysterious noxious influence to the hour of sunset. In such a climate as that of Mentone, Nice,

&c., I am persuaded the danger is merely in the sudden lowering of the temperature after sunset, which exposes to sudden chills, from the pores of the skin being often open at the time through previous exercise. As the same danger exists even in midday in passing accidentally from the sun to the shade, it is always necessary to be dressed for the latter. The invalid should inhabit a south room, and never go into a north room unless previously warmed by a fire. The one is summer, the other winter. When the weather is bad, he should make a large fire, and stay rigorously at home until it changes. Sunshine and warmth are sure soon to reappear, and thus to bring the confinement to a close. After two or three days of chilly rain, sore throats and colds begin as in England, but then the sun again shines, and they usually die away. All dinner and evening parties should be strictly forbidden. The invalid must be in by sunset, and not leave home again until the following morning. The improvement will be generally the more decided the more these rules are observed. Lastly, exercise and out-door life must not be carried so far as to produce permanent lassitude. With these precautions, the climate is safe and beneficial; without them it is unsafe and treacherous. This is evidenced by the great mortality of the natives of the Nice and Mentone districts, and of Italy generally, by pneumonia and pleurisy, two of the commonest maladies.

"'Society,' in the ordinary sense of the term, can scarcely be said to exist at Mentone. Owing, partly to the great number of invalids, and partly to the absence and expense of carriages of any kind, evening parties are very rare. From the New Year to the Carnival, the municipal authorities give balls and parties almost every week in their public rooms, and to these the foreign residents are invited, with great kindness and cordiality; indeed it has often been a source of regret to the Mentonese, that so few, of the English especially, avail themselves of these invitations. The chief intercourse is in the sketching parties and mountain excursions, for which troops of visitors, some on donkeys and some on foot, unite almost every morning in fine weather."

There is a lending library in the town chiefly of the "Tauchnitz" volumes, where the English papers may be seen. Since the following notes were written, a large new Casino and Reading-room have been commenced. Another improvement in contemplation is the "Promenade Anglaise," which will form a beautiful drive and walk along the shore in the direction of Nice, and will extend ultimately to the Cape St. Martin, two miles from the town, having trees and benches along it at intervals. The commune have now a large sum of money at their disposal for improvements, having just sold all the sea shore by auction for 36,000 francs, as far as the Ponte del Unione, the last bridge towards Nice. Part of this is to be devoted to making a public garden near the suspension bridge, on the Nice side of the town.

The Service of the Church of England is performed on the morning and afternoon of Sundays, and on every Wednesday and Friday morning throughout Lent. Several rooms have been thrown together for the purpose in an old palazzo in the town, and are capable of accomodating a large congregation. The English church however is at present situated in one of the dirtiest and narrowest lanes of Mentone, and it is proposed to build a new and larger church, for which a site has already been given, near the Pension Anglaise. The chaplain is the Rev. D. Morgan.

The principal English physician is Dr. Bennett. Dr. Maclimont is an excellent Homœopathic practitioner who frequently passes the winter at Mentone; the Italian Dr. Bottini is as highly spoken of for his skill and experience, as for the kindness and charities which have so justly endeared him to the native population.

Masters in languages are not easily found at Mentone. In music they can be more readily obtained. Mr. Edward Binyon has been induced to give lessons in drawing, and will go out sketching with his pupils.

The usual way of reaching Mentone is from Toulon, viâ Cannes and Nice, in twenty hours by diligence, or in three days by vetturino carriage, sleeping at

Vidauban and Cannes. Toulon is at present the terminus of the Mediterranean railway, and may be reached in thirty-two hours from England, but this railway will in time be continued to Genoa, and is to be completed in 1862-3, as far as Nice. This route may be varied by taking the steamer between Marseilles and Nice, or by leaving or re-seeking the railway at Aix in Provence, whence there is a branch which joins the main line at Rognac, half-way between Avignon and Marseilles. Good vetturino carriages may usually be found at the Hotel Croix d'or at Toulon, and with two or even three horses, ought never to cost more than 250 francs to Mentone, a bon-main of five francs a-day being usually expected by the driver. This sum may be much reduced by writing beforehand for one of the Cannes vetturini, who will come to meet their party at Toulon, and charge 120 francs from thence to Cannes, and 50 or 60 francs from Cannes to Mentone. The price of a place in the coupé of the diligence from Toulon to Nice is 45 francs, and from Nice to Mentone four francs. The price of a place in the banquette from Toulon to Nice is 25 francs. The price of the railway journey from Boulogne to Toulon is 145 francs in the first class, and 99 in the second. Two other routes may be taken in travelling to Mentone—one is by the beautiful Riviera road from Genoa, in 20 hours by diligence, or by a vetturino carriage in three days, the best halting places being Savona and

Oneglia. The other route brings the traveller in three days over the pass of the Col di Tenda from Turin, by vetturino carriage, or in 30 hours if he takes the diligence. This route at present obliges him to go round by Nice, the carriage road being still unfinished between Mentone and Sospello.

CONTENTS.

INTRODUCTION.

PAGE

General attractions of Mentone and its neighbourhood. Its antiquarian, geological, botanical, and artistic interest. Remains of Spanish and Saracenic in the language; Accommodation for visitors; House agent; Expenses; Trattorias and cooks; Carriages and donkeys; Climate in the winter of 1860-61. Dr. Bennett on the climate and its uses; Society; Lending Library; Promenade Anglaise; Expenses of the journey vii

FIRST IMPRESSIONS.

Journey from Nice; Arrival; Description of house, its view, and terrace; Ghost stories; Chapel of Sta. Anna and Sta. Francesca. Gateway of St. Julien; Strada Lunga; Casa Martini, and picture by Guido; Grimaldi Palace and Schools; Emigration of old families; Il Portico; Churches; Ascent to Il Cimeterio; Rue Neuve; Blessing of Pius VII.; Maison Brea; Post Office; Public Library; Church of St. John Baptist; English Church; Port and costumes; Rue St. Michel; Food; Carriages and donkeys 1

c

THE DAYS OF ST. BENOIT.

St. Benoit, the St. Swithin of Mentone; Wet weather; Drawing interruptions; Flowers; Donkey-women; the Annexation to France; Smuggling; Condition of the poor; Oranges and olives; Mademoiselle Lenoir 18

THE OLD HISTORY OF THE PRINCIPALITY.

Foundation and name of Monaco; the Roman dominion; Saracenic invasion; the championship of Giballino Grimaldi, and origin of the Genoese power; Colony from Genoa; Wars of the Guelphs and Ghibellines; Charles Grimaldi I.; Raynier; Ambroise; Jean I.; Catalan; Lambert; Jean II.; Lucien; Honorius I.; Charles II.; Hercules; Honorius II.; Louis I.; Antoine; Louise Hippolyte; Honorius III.; Honorius IV.; the French Revolution; Monaco incorporated with France; Intervention with Talleyrand in behalf of the Grimaldis; Return of the Princes; Honorius V.; rival Claimants to the throne in the Grimaldi family 28

MODERN TYRANTS AND REVOLUTIONS.

Character of Honorius V.; the protection of Monaco restored to Sardinia; Tyranny of the Prince; Increase of the taxes and customs; Confiscation of the public property; Seizure of the monopoly of commerce, and of cereales; Surveillance of the police; Taxes on agriculture; on the birth of animals; Death and epitaph of Honorius; Accession and marriage of Florestan; Demonstration of the populace; Renewed oppressions; Preparations for revolt; Mentone and Roccabruna declare themselves Free Towns; they place themselves under the protection of Sardinia; Final attempt of the Grimaldis to regain possession of their territories; Treachery of the Duke of Valentinois; Public improvements; Ten years of happiness; Mentone and Roccabruna are annexed to France; Purchase of the claims of the Prince of Monaco 41

CONTENTS. xxiii

SANTA DEVOTA AND MONACO.

Variety of foliage; Erba della Fontana; Chapelle du Bon Voyage; Custom House; Veilles; Valley of Gaumates; Chapel; Legends and festival of Santa Devota; Dance of ecclesiastics; Port of d'Hercule; Emigrés in the first revolution; Promenade St. Martin; Ancient architectural appearance of the Town; Church of Sta. Barbara; Graves of the Princes of Monaco; Gambling House; Piazza and hotels; Palace; Hall of the Grimaldis, Duke of York's room; Gardens of the Prince; Aloes; Story of the murder of Prince Lucien 56

CASTELLARE, THE CAPE ST. MARTIN, AND ROCCABRUNA.

Pine woods; Donkey cries; Position of Castellare; its architecture and inhabitants; Relics of Spanish Dominion; Return by the cemetery; Torrents of Carei and Boirigo; La Madone, its chapel and pines; Gardens of the Princes of Monaco; Garden of the Abbé St. Ambroise; Remains of the temple of Diana; Carnoles; Ponte de l'Unione; Turn to the cape; The Aristocrats' tree; Point of St. Martin; View; Pine woods and flowers; Ruins of convent; Ballad; Roccabruna, its history, legend, and situation; Castle of the Lascaris'; Church and presépe; Miracle play on the fête of Notre Dame de la Neige; The Vielle Route; Old chapel and frescoes 70

CHRISTMAS AND THE NEW YEAR.

Birth of the Bambino; Scriptural notions of the natives; Walk to the Annunziata convent; The seven lean monks; Funeral of Madame de Monleon; Decline of the old aristocracy; Change of names in the old families; Charades; Jour de l'An, and letter of Angelina Pastorelli 82

c 2

CAVALIERE TRENCA.

PAGE

His house and memorial inscription; his birth, education, and service, under the Princes of Monaco; his efforts in behalf of his country; his success, death, and burial 89

THE EASTERN ENVIRONS OF MENTONE.

The first French Revolution; Emigrants at La Cuze; Story of Monsieur le Bour; the old Riviera road; Journey of Madame de Genlis; Pont St. Louis; Story of the barbet; History of the Villa Naylor; Les Rochers Rouges; Air fountains; Dangers of the old mule road; Palazzo Orenga; Signor Granducci; St. Mauro; Grimaldi; Ciotti Inferiòre; Ciotti Superiore 96

GORBIO AND ST. AGNESE.

The valley of Gorbio, town and views; Festa; Walk from Gorbio to Roccabruna; Ascent to St. Agnese, village, church, and terrazone; Story of the Saracenic castle; Festa of St. Agnese; Sta. Lucia; Wolves in the mountains 104

VENTIMIGLIA, BORDIGHERA, AND DOLCEACQUA.

Italian appearance of Ventimiglia; Cathedral and palace of the Lascaris; View from the Roya; Church of St. Michaele; Borgo di Ventimiglia; Escape of Francesco Novello at Ventimiglia; Road to Bordighera; Bridge over the Nervia; Bordighera described in Dr. Antonio; Palm groves; First carriage accident on the precipices; Eve of St. Mauro; Second accident on the precipices; Fête of St. Mauro; Church of St. Agostino; Excursion to Dolceacqua; Campo Rosso; Romanesque church and cemetery; Town and Castle of the Dorias 111

TURBIA, LAGHETTO, AND ESA.

The Trophæa Augusti, history and remains; The "Written Rocks"; Colonna del Ré; Ravine of Laghetto; Convent; Ex-votos and sacred image; Pilgrimages; History of the shrine; Abdication of Charles Albert at Laghetto; Origin of the name;—the Saracenic town of Esa 124

IL GRAN' MONDO.

Inferiority of the Berceau to the Gran' Mondo; Difficulties of the ascent; View from the summit; Descent; Dangers and darkness 134

MONTI AND THE GOOURG DI L'ORA.

The Via della Pietra Scritta; Reminisences of La Catarina; Church of Monti; Excursion to the cascade of the Goourg di l'Ora; Story of the English philosopher; the Grotta del Eremito; Return by Castellare 140

THE CARNIVAL AND LENT.

Invasion of masks; Balls and vaudevilles; Street masquers; Pic Nic at La Madone; The gift of paradise; Ballad ... 144

CASTIGLIONE AND GHIANDOLA.

Mentonese proverb; Ascent to Castiglione; its position; Architecture and inhabitants; Descent by Monti; Excursion to Sospello and Ghiandola; Breglio 151

ON DONKEYS TO PEGLIA.

Ascent by St. Agnese; Theresine bribed: Arid mountains; First View of Peglia, its church and architecture; Hospitality of inhabitants; Return in the dark by Gorbio 157

EXCURSION TO NICE AND PEGLIONE.

Potervium; Villafranca and its history; Nice, its situation and scenery; The castle, Croix de Marbre,—and houses of Massena and Garibaldi; Ascent of the olive woods; Pin de Bellet; St. Romain; The Seven Villages; St. Jannet; St. Pons; Chateau St. André; Grotto of Falicon; Ruined town of Chateauneuf; Tourette; Cimies; Temple of Diana; Tino delle Fade; Legends of Maison Garin; Franciscan Convent; Winged Crucifix; Dust of Nice; Drap; Fontaine de Giallier; Story of Lady Bute; Story of Ray Mill; Wonderful position of Peglione,—its views and architecture; Ascent of Mont Agel 162

PASSION WEEK AND EASTER.

Rejoicings of the natives over the end of Lent; Ceremonies of Palm Sunday; "The King of Glory shall come in"; grinding Judas's Bones; Jesu lié; Ceremonies of Holy Thursday; Washing of the feet; Good Friday; Funeral ceremonies; The Pilgrim Preacher of the Riviera; Easter Sunday 172

AN EXCURSION IN APRIL.

Drive to San Remo; The story of the palm trees; Monks; Doria palace; Statue of God the Father; Hospital for leprosy; Walk to St. Romano; Excursion to Taggia; its streets and architecture; House of Signor Ruffini; of Signora Eleanora; of "La Marchesa"; Bridge and shrine; Ascent to Castellaro; Description of Lampedusa from Dr. Antonio; Diligence to Porto Maurizio; Carriage to Albenga; Towers; Cathedral and baptistery; L'Albergo d'Italia; Expedition to Garlanda; its valley, its church, and its Domenichino; A primitive luncheon; Pietra; Finale; Savona; Expedition to Il Santuario, its legend and relics; Savona cathedral by lamp-light; Night travelling; Arrival

CONTENTS. xxvii

PAGE

at Genoa; English church; The Acqua Sole; Ancient cloister and streets; Dickens' description of Genoa; Piazza St. Matteo; Rogers' description of it; best views of Genoa; Excursion to Porto Fino; Albaro; Nervi; Camoglie; Ruta; Day at Porto Fino and Piccolo Paggi; Return by Albaro and Sta. Margherita; Journey to Piacenza; its Piazza and Cathedral; St. Donino; Parma; its cathedral, baptistery and palace; Modena; its cathedral and palace; Rapid return to Mentone; Expenses 178

FAREWELLS.

Scramble to the Claudian Castle; Ride to Santa Lucia; Last words 203

A. Adlard, Lith

A Winter at Mentone.

FIRST IMPRESSIONS.

Dec. 1st.

"How did you get over the precipices?" is generally the first question asked of any one who arrives at Mentone, and in our case it was a real subject of congratulation, that we arrived with unbroken necks, for the hour, the weather, and the driver had alike been favorable to an accident. We left Nice so late, that night had begun to close in before we reached the summit of the Turbith, as the mountain is called, which divides that township from this, and the last glimmer of daylight deserted us, whilst our horses were tearing at full gallop along its fearful ledges, with a driver who delighted in showing off, by keeping as close as possible to the edge of the precipice. The said driver, as we left our hotel at Nice, had put his head in at the window at the last moment, with ominous shakings and mutterings of, "Nous aurons les eaux à passer, Monsieur, il y aura beaucoup d'eau," but we believed these threats were founded on fiction, till just as we reached the plain and were reposing on the belief in danger past, we were roused up to danger present, by the carriage being suddenly brought to a stop, amid shouts of "Les eaux, les eaux"; a sound of rushing waters, and an indistinct vision in the faint starlight, of a broad, white, foaming torrent, which was raging across the road in front of us, and carrying everything before it. The driver declared his belief that the carriage could not possibly pass the flood, and certainly not with us in it; so we all had to turn out in the pouring rain, into the swimming, slippery road. Happily, however, though its parapet had been washed away, a little foot-bridge of broken planks, still remained standing just above the water, across which we were able to walk, while the carriage and horses contrived to splash round through the shallows higher up the river, without being overturned. When the flood was passed, lights streaming through a misty street, announced that we had reached Mentone; but then began the new difficulty of finding our house, for we had taken a house beforehand, as we had been induced to believe the reports which Mentonese house-owners circulate, that every apartment is let at the beginning of the season, even when two-thirds of their houses are standing empty, and half their windows displaying placards of "Apartements à louer." Not a single person we met seemed to be able to distinguish any house in the place by its name, certainly no one in the crowded street confessed to knowing Maison Trenca, as our house is called; and when, after endless search, one individual was discovered who had heard of such a place, it was only to tell us that there were two Maisons Trenca, and thus to create a new source of bewilderment. We could only drive on in the darkness to the Genoa end of the town, where on one side of the road the sea was roaring beneath a stone causeway, while on the other, lights twinkled far up in the quaint overhanging buildings. Here, after storming two wrong houses in turn, and disappointing a strange family who were anxiously expecting their own friends, and who rushed out, with arms extended to embrace them, we at length discovered our future abode, high on the side of a steep olive-clad hill, to be reached by a narrow stony way, which wound up behind a little chapel, where a lamp was glimmering over a gloomy altar, and which we have since found to be dedicated to St. Anne, and to have a very quaint Turkish appearance. The road was so narrow that it was all we could do to get our driver to venture on the ascent, but at last, on some workmen assuring him that a turn existed further on, and that he would not be obliged to remain jammed up there for life as he expected, he was induced to urge his horses up the hill and set us down at our own gate.

Our apartment is a fair specimen of most others we have seen in Mentone. It is on the first floor, with a bright salon looking towards the garden, having glass doors opening on a balcony. The salle-à-manger only looks out on the olive wood behind, and is less cheerful, but the three bedrooms and the kitchen are excellent. All the rooms except one, overlook a vast expanse of blue sea, above groves of magnificent olive trees, and from the garden a scent of fresh flowers is wafted up, even in this beginning of December. From this garden the peaks of the Berceau Mountain are seen rising above the thickets of oranges and lemons, and beyond, a chain of rose-coloured rocks descending in an abrupt precipice to the blue waters of the bay, while on the furthest promontory, Bordighera (the scene of Dr. Antonio) gleams white in the sunshine. Twice a day, a lovely fairy vision salutes us, first, when in the sunrise, Corsica reveals itself across the sapphire water, appearing so distinctly that you can count every ravine and indentation of its jagged mountains, and feel as if a small boat would easily carry you over to it in an hour; and again, in the evening, when as a white ghost, scarcely distinguishable from the clouds around it, and looking inconceivably distant, it looms forth dimly in the yellow sunset. Bordighera is also sometimes the subject of a curious aërial phenomenon, when the town and houses are separated from the sea by an effect of mirage, and seem to be lifted up and suspended in mid-air.

We have had some difficulty in obtaining a native servant, the maid we first tried to engage having refused to take service in this part of the place on account of her terror of passing the little chapel of St. Anne, the burial place of the Gastaldy family, which is close to our gate, and which the peasants say is haunted by a " Revenant," who walks from thence every midnight, as far as the chapel of Sta. Francesca, which is also close to us. A Mentonese accounted for the superstition by a story that the man who used to light the lamp, which burns nightly in the chapel, had a particular grudge against a priest, who was obliged to pass that way every night, and who was notorious for neglecting to fulfil his duties towards the sick. One night the lamplighter concealed himself here, and as the priest passed the chapel, he heard an awful voice from its interior exclaim, "I wished, dear friend, to have seen you before I died, but as you would not come to me then, now I have come to you." The priest, who imagined that he recognized the voice of a dead and neglected Gastaldy, was so dreadfully frightened, that he set off " au plein galop," and did not rest till he found himself safe in the Cathedral of Ventimiglia, five miles distant.

The Mentonese natives are full of superstitions, and invest each house and rock with some terrible story.

Most of these have their origin in some actual horror, of which the facts have been forgotten except by a few of the older and better class of inhabitants, while the impression remains universal, and causes the spot to be avoided or looked upon with suspicion. Thus one of the haunted houses is said to be that of Monsieur Joseph de Monleon. This was once a cemetery, or at least the place where French soldiers were buried who died in the hospital of Mentone. It is said that several of these were interred before the last breath had fairly deserted them, and that some were even heard to groan and cry out afterwards. A gentleman who is still living in the plaee, remembers passing the cemetery as a child, on the way to school, and seeing over the wall a French Grenadier, who had been buried alive the evening before, and had still strength enough left to drag himself out of the trench into which he was thrown; he was sitting on its edge, waiting for daylight, and for some one to pass by and come to his assistance, but the women, who had heard him call out as they went to the fields, had taken him for a ghost, and had fled in terror, instead of going to help him. Another curious anecdote has led to the sea-shore in a particular direction being avoided after dark. In the year 1793, or '94, when the French troops were passing through Mentone, they bivouacked in the Avenue St. Roch, where numbers of Hussars lay down to sleep beneath the trees by the wayside. One of them, who had the care of the kitchen, began meantime to cut down branches from the trees to feed his fire, and one of the branches falling on the nose of a sleeper, awoke him to furious anger and abuse; a violent quarrel ensued, and the men, drawing their swords, fought on the sea-shore, in front of the place where the Hotel des Quatres Nations now stands. Here they were both so overcome with rage, that they stabbed each other, and fell dead at the same moment, when the spectators, hurried away by their regimental duties, hastily placed each in a corn-sack, and having scooped out holes in the sand, buried them as they were. A few days after, a washerwoman, hanging out her clothes to dry on this spot, in a high wind, saw a piece of cord blown up from the sand. She pulled at it, and with such force, that she drew up the sack which was attached to it, from which the head of one of the soldiers jumped up, and regarded her fixedly. Overwhelmed with terror, and crying out that she saw a spirit, she fainted away. The people, who ran to her assistance, disinterred the poor soldiers for burial elsewhere, and the story is generally forgotten, but the idea of something terrible connected with that spot has never been eradicated. While ideas of this kind attach themselves to extinct burial places, it is not to be wondered at that the actual cemetery of present times possesses its local terrors. As the clock strikes midnight, a procession of gigantic "revenants" is believed to issue from its portals, and to march solemnly, two and two, along the adjoining terrace, till at a particular turn in the path, they all vanish into air, no one knows how; still, it must be confessed, that when some young Mentonese gentlemen summoned courage, a short time ago, to watch the cemetery gates all night, they came home in the morning very much disappointed at not having seen the ghostly procession, but also rather—relieved.

The terrace below our house is an inexhaustible delight, as it presents a new picture at every turn, framed in the gnarled trunks of its olive trees. Here is the chapel of Santa Francesca, which contains the tomb of a M. Richelmy, officer in the guard of the Prince of Monaco, "Helas! trop tôt enlevé, de la plus tendre affection de sa sœur inconsolable." A portrait of the young guardsman hangs above his grave, but has decayed equally with the mouldering flowers on the altar, which is always covered with an embroidered white cloth. At the western extremity of the terrace is the town, which rises from the sea in tier above tier of the quaintest, tallest, and most varied houses imaginable. It is entered by the old gateway of St. Julien, with a fountain beside it, where any one who wishes to study costume and colour, had better stand to watch the water-carriers in the morning. Above it a ruined wall runs up the rocks to join an old tower near the cemetery, which is said to be a remnant of the Mediæval Castle of Poggio-Pino, a stronghold of the Counts of Ventimiglia, and a fortress of celebrity long before Mentone sprang into existence.

The gateway leads into the Strada Lunga, the narrowest of possible streets, all arches and gutters and dirt, with shirts, stockings, and other garments, mingled with sheep-skins and goat-skins, hanging out to dry on ropes, slung across from one high upper window to another. This street, till quite modern days, was *the* great street of the town, and it is remembered how before the first French revolution, the ladies of Mentone used to sit out and work in the open air, just as the peasants do now, before the doors of the houses, or (one is expected to say) the "palaces" of the Rue Longue. A contemporary letter describes the "animated appearance" which this gave to the place in those days, the gentlemen stopping to chat with each group as they passed. "Towards evening, all the society walked out to the Cape St. Martin, to drink coffee and play at games, under the Aristocrat's Tree," and the nights were enlivened by frequent serenades, which were given by their admirers beneath the windows of the principal belles. At that time the town consisted only of this street, and a few of the narrow alleys which surround the principal church, and it was shut in by two gateways, one, that of St. Julien, which still remains, the other situated where Amarante's Bazaar now stands. Continuing our walk through the town— one of the first houses on the left of the Strada Lunga, No. 133, is entered by a picturesque old doorway, surmounted by a niche, containing a little brown image of the Virgin, and marked with the date 1543. This is the abode of the Martini family, who have inhabited it ever since its foundation. Three hundred years ago one of its members fell in love with a beautiful Roman lady, the daughter of a Cavaliere Paliarci, and when they were married, the bride brought with her to Mentone, as her dowry, a picture of the Virgin, which has always had the reputation of being a Guido. The family of Martini were then powerful and rich, but they are now fallen and poor, for most of their property was lost during the revolution, and almost all its members were forced to emigrate and take refuge at Genoa; only an old aunt was left behind, and while she was taking a last look round the house, to see if there was anything she could secrete before it was seized and turned into a gendarmerie, she espied the Madonna of the bridal Paliarci, and hid it. When the Emigrés returned from exile, the old aunt was dead, and the picture was supposed to have been destroyed, till one day it was accidentally found, hidden in a hole in the wall, but a good deal injured; the glass which covered it having been broken, which had caused a large cut across the face of the Madonna. The picture still hangs on the wall of a dismal chamber in the old house, where it may be seen, on application to its venerable proprietor, Monsieur Martini, and where it is now the sole ornament, so that its beauty is enhanced tenfold by the poverty-stricken appearance of all that surrounds it. It is a small head of the Madonna, looking upwards in a halo of light, in which the colouring is still fresh, and the execution soft and delicate. Many years ago old Monsieur Martini was offered a sum of 4000 francs for it, which he then refused, but now he would have no objection to part with this interesting family relic for that, or even a smaller sum.

Near this house, still on the left, is another building distinguished by its heavy projecting cornices, resting on carved stone corbels. This was formerly the Palace of that branch of the Grimaldi family, which maintained a separate government in Mentone, and afterwards of the Grimaldi Princes of the Monaco, when the rest of the family ceded their rights, and Mentone was re-united to the Mother State. It is said to have been built from the materials of the old castle of Poggio-Pino. The staircase is handsome, with a coved ceiling, and a marble pillar at its foot; and at the back of the Palace, which overhangs the quay, by looking over the wall on the edge of the sea, the remains of the steps may still be seen cut in the rock below, by which the Princes descended to the water. The chambers are now used as schools, "Ecoles primaires," the expenses of which are paid by the commune, neither boys nor girls themselves paying anything.

Entering the school, you find three pleasant-looking French Sœurs de Charité in their nun's dress, who teach in three separate rooms. The largest is appropriated to the infant class, which is ranged on steps, before which their teacher stands, while the children follow her in singing, and in different manual exercises. The little creatures do it with much vivacity, and their actions are full of native grace and freedom. A little boy of three years old is called up, and makes a bow and "bonjour," with as great courtesy as a nobleman. The copy books exhibited are wonderfully well written, if they are really "first books," as the nuns say. The inner room is given up to the first class of bigger girls, at work on "broderie." While thus occupied, they repeat a kind of Litany, in which the main subject is rapidly muttered by the Sister, who never raises her eyes from the artificial flowers she is making, so that the children do just as they like, and not a symptom of reverence is evinced, either during the repetition of the endless titles with which the Virgin is saluted, or during the "Ora pro nobis," which comes between each of them. When work is done, books (a short abridgment of Sacred History) are taken out, and one or two come up to read, the rest play, or read as they please. Nothing can be less edifying or instructive than this part of the education, justifying the assertion of Marie, a maid in this house, that "they learn nothing." The sisters, however, both like and are liked by the children, who they consider to be far more teachable than those in France, and with whose quickness and intelligence they are much astonished. They come from Aix, in Provence, and have only just been installed in the place of the former teachers, the Italian nuns. When asked if they understood patois, "Oh, no," they said, "but signs do just as well."

Many of the old Mentone families who formerly lived in this street, and who were attached to Italian goverment and customs, have emigrated, since the annexation, to other towns on the Riviera, where they can be under the Sardinian rule. Among these, the old family of Clairvoisin has just removed to St. Remo in despair at the annexation, having lived here from time immemorial. From being grandees of the land, they were reduced to the rank of peasants; but they still preserved a chain of family portraits, unbroken from the year 1060; their china was Majolica, embossed with the family arms, and their furniture magnificent from age and carving. Before they left Mentone their house was thrown open to the public and many people went to see the antiquities contained in it, which would readily have found purchasers, but when asked if they would sell them, the Clairvoisins proudly replied, "No, they might be peasants now, but were not these their family relics?"

Lower down this street, near "Il Portico," is the ascent to the principal churches of the town, by a handsome flight of broad steps, paved with a Mosaic of small stones, which was repaired and beautified four years ago by the voluntary exertions of the inhabitants of the narrow street at its foot. At the top is a broad platform, overlooking the bay and the red rocks, with the promontories of Ventimiglia and Bordighiera. On one side is the large and handsome parish church of St. Michaele, decorated with a smart statue of that saint, in a Roman helmet, and fly-away costume, trampling on the devil. Over the inside of the door is a curious old Giottesque picture of saints. The other church, prettily covered all over with delicate stucco work, is dedicated to La Santissima Conceptione. Opposite St. Michaele is the Hospital, attended by French Sisters of Charity. The picturesque gateway by the side of it, with the dark winding flights of steps seen beneath, leads up to the cemetery on the hill top. On the church steps, in the narrow street, sotto Il Portico, and everywhere else in Mentone, you are saluted by the characteristic cries of the donkey-drivers, and jostled by the donkies themselves, which are the regular household servants of the place, and are used to bring down the olives from the mountains, to carry manure back instead, to tread in the wine press, to work in the mills, to bring fuel, to rock the little children in their gently swaying panniers, to supply milk for the babies, and so on ad infinitum, till at last they die of over-work, or old age, and are eaten up in sausages.

The universal burial place of Mentone is the Cemetery, which forms the top of the pyramid-like town, and looks like a castle in the distance. Funerals generally take place at night, because the streets are then much quieter, and the processions are most picturesque, conducted by the two burial confraternities of the "Penitents noirs et blancs," who issue from the parish church and wind up through the steep streets, with lighted candles or torches in their hands, all the mourners and followers bearing lighted candles also, which they extinguish when the body arrives at the gate of the cemetery; after which it is frequently left in a little chapel for several days before actual interment. The rich who wish to have a monument, can buy a piece of ground; but the poor are buried in the centre of the cemetery under little mounds, while small wooden crosses mark their place of interment. A plot of ground inside the wall has been set aside for the Protestant burial place; but at present it only contains a few graves, one being that of a young lady who was killed by a dreadful accident near the Pont St. Louis.

At the end of the Rue Longue is the entrance to the Rue Neuve, where, from a terraced garden on the right, Pope Pius VII. blessed the people on his return to Rome, after his long exile in France; all the changeable inhabitants, who a few years before had raged against ecclesiastical power, and publicly burnt his predecessor in effigy, having now flocked together with one mind and one voice to do him honour.

An inscription on the wall tells how

Pio VII. P.M.
Lutetia Romam redux
Hinc
Cælestem populo supplici
Benedictionem impertibat
Die XI. Mensis Februarii
An. Dom. MDCCCXIII.

Opposite this, on the Maison Brea is another of those house inscriptions, which render a street walk in Italy so interesting, and which are so much needed in England, to mark for posterity, the dwellings of our good and illustrious dead.

" Au General Brea,
Né a Menton le 23 Avril, 1720.
Mort à Paris le 24 Juin, 1848.
Pour la defense de l'ordre
et de la patrie.

Par decret du grand conseil des
Villes libres de Menton et Roquebrune
du 25 Septembre, 1848."

Close to this is the Mairie, where the Syndic and Municipal Council transact the business of the town. Here is preserved one of the stones of the Bastile, which were sent at the time of its destruction to every commune in France, but which, for the most part, have been since destroyed. Here also is a public library, which came to the town three years ago by a bequest of Madame Villarney, neé Sassi. It is open to the public from nine to twelve o'clock, and from two till four, but as yet it is not well organized; there are neither chairs nor tables, the room is cold and wretched, and you may not take any of the books away. The library consists chiefly of medical works. Adjoining the Mairie is the church of St. John Baptist, dark and gloomy, with a horrid picture of the bloody head of the saint.

The English church is approached by the filthiest of alleys, winding down from a little Piazza at the entrance of the town, on the Genoa side. It is generally said that the building itself was once a palace of the Princes of Monaco, but this is not the case; it was built by the Alboni family, and formerly inhabited by the "Podestat" or "Intendente," an office which was suppressed in 1792. It still retains traces of its former magnificence, entirely out of character with the wretched buildings which surround it. The staircase has the pillar at its foot, and the coved ceiling, so often found in old Italian palaces, and over what were once the chimney pieces, are two old portraits of Grimaldis. These are now swathed in red calico by the church authorities, who have also exiled all the other old pictures to a dark cupboard, and caused the ceilings, which were once covered with frescoes, to be whitewashed. The noise of the sea, by which the building is begirt on two sides, is often very disturbing to the service.

Most of the alleys near this lead out to the Port, crammed with picturesque shipping, or to the Fort, a little yellow wave-beaten castle, only connected with the mainland by a kind of pier, which blazes like liquid gold against the blue mountains in the sunset. Hence you have beautiful views on either side; on the right towards the olive-clad hill sprinkled with English villas, which has the shining peak of Berceau rising above it, while beyond are the precipices of the Rochers Rouges, the castle of Ventimiglia on its rock, and brilliant palm-girt Bordighera on the furthest point of the promontory. On the left are the port and shipping, with the flat table-topped Mount Agel, the bold crag of the Tête du Chien, and the Cape St. Martin green with olive gardens and pines, running far out into the sea. Picturesque bits of costume may sometimes be found in the port, especially amongst the fishermen, some of whom may chance to have landed from the smaller and less modernized towns of the Riviera. Their brilliant scarlet caps, or sometimes only scarlet knobs rising from a broad band of black or brown, are always picturesque; but the chief characteristic costume here is the large flat white hat, the general head-dress of the female peasantry, of great use in supporting the heavy burdens, which they carry on their heads. These hats are composed of straw, very thick and very tightly sewn together with strong white thread, in such quantities that they have a white appearance; they are exceedingly heavy, but they are also very durable. The better class of peasantry always wear them adorned with black velvet strings, or sometimes with stars of black velvet sewn round the top, and all wear a coloured handkerchief beneath, which is tied under the chin, and which is still worn when the hat is taken off.

The principal street of Mentone is the Rue St. Michel. Here is situated Amarante's Bazaar, a most useful place, where almost everything may be obtained, and with the exception of the native wood-work, at not unreasonable prices. Almost opposite this, is the family house of the Trencas, on the face of which a marble slab bears an inscription in memory of the Chevalier Trenca, the most distinguished modern citizen of Mentone. Behind the Bazaar, is the Maison D'Adhemar, a dilapidated Palazzo, surrounding a small court yard, where the brother of Robespierre lived, as the representative of the people during the French Revolution. Here, too, Napoleon frequently visited a friend who occupied the ground floor: he passed through Mentone several times as General, and occupied the house now inhabited by M. Grasse, and used as a Pharmacie. In this street are the principal hotels, the Turin, Vittoria, and the Quatres Nations. In front of the Hotel Turin is a fountain with a tawdry bust of the present Emperor, put up at the time of the annexation. On the right is the shop of the English grocer, Mr. Willoughby, who is the first person every one sees on arriving at Mentone, for he is the house agent, and always appears with the inventory; besides which you hear of him morning, noon, and night afterwards, as he is the receiver-general of all the little commissions of English masters and the little troubles of English servants. At the end of the Rue St. Michel, near the little chapel of St. Roch, is the house called the "Maison Gastaldy," one of the largest of those that are let in separate suites of apartments to the English.

At first we thought we ran a risk of being starved, as good cooks are difficult to find, besides being very expensive, and the Pension Anglaise, which we tried first, sent us scarcely enough for one person, for the same sum which had procured a first-rate dinner for four, both at Rome and Lucca; but we have at length discovered a restaurant, from whence we get a dinner which is very tolerable, after it has been stripped of its oil and garlic, and has had some extra cooking bestowed upon it by our own servants. Almost everything that grows is eaten here, including the bitter Coruba beans, which are a favorite food with children, some of whom, when asked if they really liked them, replied, " Oh si, quello que è buono per l'altri è buono per Christiani." The donkeys after their regular food, have a dessert of lemons and bran, just as we should have of oranges and biscuits. Cows and sheep too are frequently fed upon lemons, which they like exceedingly. Meat at Mentone is always as hard as stone, which is not to be wondered at, as the unfortunate flocks, which have no lemons, are constantly pastured on the sea-shore, where they can have little except stones to eat.

The charges for carriages are very high. No carriage even with one horse is allowed to go out at all under six francs; for a drive to Monaco or Ventimiglia the charge is twelve francs for two horses, and fifteen francs for the whole day; twenty francs is often asked for going to Bordighera, but fifteen is taken. On this account the richer visitors find it cheaper and pleasanter to hire a carriage from Nice for the season, and the poorer content themselves with donkeys; these are also more expensive at Mentone than at Nice, the charges being two francs for half the day, or three francs for the whole day, including the guide, a day being supposed to begin at 9 a.m. and to end at 6 p.m.

The easiest way of obtaining money is through a banker at Nice, who upon a letter of credit will forward any sum required in a parcel by the Messageries Imperiales.

THE DAYS OF ST. BENOIT.

Mentone, Dec. 10.

It has poured with rain almost ever since we came, but "if it rains on St. Benoit," say the inhabitants, (which unfortunately it did) "it will rain more or less for forty days, and then it will be fine weather." So since we have discovered that St. Benoit is the Mentonese St. Swithin, we have lived upon hope, and have learnt to make the best of the few fine days which trespass upon his property. The extreme wet has caused endless "eboulements," and the other day our next neighbour's garden slipped bodily down in the night towards the sea, carrying all its earth, shrubs and orange trees with it. The diligences and the mails come in twelve hours after their time, and the postman often takes fright at the state of the elements, and refuses altogether to carry round the letters, or turns back when half way to his destination, so that one of our friends has taken to giving him wine on the days when he does appear by way of encouragement for the future. Francoise, our new maid, declares that she *must* be half an hour late in the morning, it takes her so long to pick up her things, and splash from stone to stone in the broken pavement of the street; and in the English church the service is much interrupted, and the congregation almost deafened by the noise of the sea.

We have employed all the gleams of morning sunshine in drawing the old gateway from the terrace in spite of the persecution of a crowd of children, who as soon as we have sat down quietly, and are beginning to get on with our work, have invented the new torment of dancing round in a circle, and singing in a chorus—

> Monsieur pinta, pinta, pinta,
> Vede, vede, vede, ve ..! ...!!

This poetic turn would be amusing, if they would confine themselves, as they sometimes do, to addressing each other, putting the commonest things quite naturally into rhyme. A quaint little toddle called Tain is a general recipient of these improvisations, and I have heard quite a commonplace call for this little object, which might be translated thus:

> "Little Tain, little Tain,
> Will you never come again;
> Oh! you funny little Tain
> Do not let us call in vain."

Sometimes our sufferings are varied by having sand poured into our paint boxes, or little stones thrown at our heads. On these occasions, the mothers who will stand looking on quite unmoved for their own part highly applaud our taking vengeance for ourselves. But the other day, when one piece of earth after another had come tumbling down at intervals upon my book from the rocks above, and at last out of all patience, I rushed after the supposed children, and finding my tormentors only to be cocks and hens scratching over my head, turned my vengeance upon them; the owner was perfectly furious, and rushed at me, screaming and quivering with rage, "What, are not the hens to take their walks upon the rocks? are not the hens to be allowed to amuse themselves? how could I dare to drive away the hens, who were a great deal better than myself? for did not they know how to lay eggs, which was really useful, while I could do nothing but cover a piece of paper with paint?"

The beauty of the flowers still in bloom in the gardens astonishes us increasingly. On our terrace we have the tall light blue and the scarlet Salvia, waving Tobacco plant, and Parma violets which flower all the year round. Besides these, there are various sorts of Tropæolum, the Mimosa, large flowering Senna, and the Castor Oil plant, with its prickly crimson balls and large leaves like those of a Plane tree. The principal wild flower now in bloom is a kind of small Arum, which the natives call Cappuchini, or else Lampe Romane, from its resemblance to those articles when turned upside down; this quite covers the terraces under the olive trees. Our maid Francoise turns out to have some wonderful garden " chez elle," which admits of her constantly bringing us presents of fresh oranges and lemons, and this morning she gave us a splendid bunch of large white Jessamine in full bloom.

We had not been here long before several donkey-women presented themselves to secure our custom. We engaged ourselves to a wild Meg Merrilies figure in a broad white hat, with a red handkerchief tied underneath, and a bunch of flowers stuck jauntily in the side of her hair. She rejoices in the name of Theresina Ravellina Muratori de Buffa; but though her second name was only improvised by herself because she did not think her other three sufficiently distinctive, she is generally known as "La Ravellina," in order to distinguish her from another and far more charming old Theresine (Paturine) who also keeps donkeys, and who is familiar with every story of the place, from the oldest fairy legend, to the details of the sufferings under the late Princes of Monaco. Our Theresine too, chatters incessantly, though in a less interesting way. The first day she went with us, she displayed all the various articles of her apparel, which had been gifts from divers English ladies, who had been "toujours contentes de Ravelline," evidently in the hope that we should also add to her wardrobe on the "jour de l'an." When we asked her how many sons she had, she told us she had three, one was a sailor, one was a donkey boy, and the third was no longer anything, "parce que le bon Dieu l'avait enlevé." We afterwards discovered that " La Ravelline," has a philosophy of her own; when one's friends die, she says, "Il ne faut pas se facher, ça perds le temps, parce qu' on sait toujours qu' il faut mourir." Thus, she said, it was when her first husband died, it was the will of God that he should die, and so instead of complaining she married a Milanese; the only real misfortune was that her second husband's trade was cutting trenches for drainage in the olive gardens, and as this cannot be done in bad weather they were sometimes very ill off; "mais le bon Dieu le veut, il ne faut pas se facher."

Every one here is full of the French annexation, and indeed it is difficult to imagine what can have induced the people to vote for a change, after nine happy years of freedom under the government of Sardinia. It is said to be entirely owing to the Syndic, whose French wife gave him French tendencies, although he had been appointed under the Sardinian government. A poor man on the mountains on being asked how they could thus voluntarily enslave themselves, gave a more simple explanation the other day in his "Ah! Signor, ... Citroni"! It was probably really the case that the hope of a greater facility for the fruit trade induced the Mentonese to be led by one or two persons into joining themselves to France. Now they have found out their mistake, and bitterly repent it, for not only is Mentone liable to French conscription, and beset with fresh difficulties in the exportation of its lemons, but Pollenta, which is one of the chief articles of consumption among the lower orders (who could not change their diet with their nationality) is taxed one sous the litra, and costs six sous here, while in Italy, only one-mile-and-a-half distant, it only costs five. All this leads to a great deal of smuggling; and the other day as we were coming home by the Italian Custom House, our donkey woman stopped before a little old Cabaret just on the other side of the frontier, and called loudly, "Rufina, Rufina," upon which a young woman came out, and after long whispering presented her with a small parcel, which she hid mysteriously in the bosom of her dress. It was "a little commission," she said; but after we were safe across the frontier, where she ostentatiously exhibited the contents of our basket to the gendarmes who were on the watch, she revealed that the packet contained tobacco, (cheaper in Italy, like almost everything else) which she had undertaken to convey to the town, in the same place she quaintly added, "where many pieces of lace and other articles had travelled before it."

Compared with the state of the English poor, there is very little real poverty here; almost every one has some little olive ground or orange garden which they can call their own. Old Theresine told us that when young men marry, they sometimes begin life with nothing; then the first object of the married pair always is to put themselves "à l'abri," and not to be dependant upon hired lodgings, for which they might be called on to pay rent just when it would be most difficult for them to do so. For this purpose they hoard up till they have got 400 or 500 francs, for which sum a house may be bought in the upper part of the town, between the cemetery and St. Michaele. The house secured, the next thing to be bought is a piece of rock, which by perseverance and hard labour may, in this climate, soon be transformed into a fruitful garden. Here they often labour all night long, and lights are to be seen glimmering and songs heard from the orange gardens of the poor all through the dark hours. The first year they carry up earth, prepare the ground, and plant wild orange and lemon trees; the second year they graft them, and the third year they begin to reap the fruits. The oranges and lemons require watering once a week all through the summer, but the olives require more than this. They have to be constantly trenched round to give air to the roots, without which they do not flourish, and once a year (in March and April) they require to be manured with rags, which are very expensive.* During the rag season the smell from the olive groves is most unpleasant, and the effluvia from the ships, which convey the rags to Mentone, is so offensive, that unloading them becomes a service of the greatest danger.

We have now made several pleasant acquaintances amongst the native inhabitants, of whom we had already heard much from a friend who had lived here for many years.

---

* "A circular trench, about a foot deep and two feet wide, is dug round the trunk, and in this the rags, mostly procured in bales from Naples, are laid; a curious assemblage of shreds of cloth gaiters, sleeves of jackets, bits of blankets, horse-rugs, and so forth—the whole conveying an uncomfortable idea of a Lazzarone's cast off clothes. A quantity not exceeding twenty pounds English weight is allotted to each tree, and then the earth, which had been displaced for their reception, is thrown over them, and they are left to ferment and gradually decompose. Some agriculturalists throw a layer of common manure over the rags before covering them with earth, but many experienced persons contend that this is unnecessary. Great precaution is requisite to prevent any blight from settling on the leaves."— *(Mrs. Gretton.)*

"To whom do the upper classes in Mentone owe their general knowledge and intelligence about everything," I asked of her one day.

"Oh, to Mademoiselle Lenoir," was the reply.

"Where did they get their strong religious feeling and ready discernment of right and wrong?"

"It came from Mademoiselle Lenoir."

"What leads people to be so charitable in Mentone, and to take so much trouble to prevent any poverty among their poorer neighbours"?

"It is owing to Mademoiselle Lenoir."

"Where do people go in the afternoon, as they turn up the narrow street where the Mairie is, and stop at a house there?"

"They go to consult Mademoiselle Lenoir."

"And how did this lady gain this great influence"?

"By love."

"Then how active and strong Mademoiselle Lenoir must be."

"No, Mademoiselle Lenoir has been bed-ridden for two years."

"How then has she been able to carry on all her good works"?

"By love."

"Is she very rich"?

"No, she is very poor indeed, she has scarcely anything."

"How does she live then"?

"Oh, Mademoiselle Lenoir lives on love."

After hearing all this, I naturally longed to see this lady who had done so much for the place, who was so loving and so beloved, and whose sick chamber is like a shrine, where people go for assistance and advice. Soon I had a message to say that she would be willing and able to receive me.

Twenty-two years ago, Mademoiselle Lenoir, who had spent many years in Russia as a governess, came to Mentone intending only to spend a short time there. During the time she had intended to stay, however, she saw enough of the ignorance which prevailed, and its effects upon the character of the people, to touch her deeply. For herself, she was then young, strong, energetic, and highly educated. She had no particular object left in life, and her aged mother, the only near relative she had in the world, was willing to make a home with her wherever she wished, so she was determined to devote her life to a work which seemed to her to have been especially thrown in her way, when other occupations failed. When she arrived at Mentone, the upper classes were in a state of almost heathen darkness and ignorance, the men merely careless and mindless, the women engrossed with dress and frivolities, both without taste or acquirements, and her impression was that raising *their* minds through education, would be the easiest and surest means of obtaining a good influence over the lower classes afterwards, and thus raising the standard both of intellect and morality throughout Mentone. So she opened a school, which at first contained only three pupils, but which all the young gentry of Mentone afterwards considered it their greatest happiness to attend. The foundation of all her teaching was love, and whilst she poured out the treasures of her own richly-stored mind to her scholars, love was the ruling principle of action, which it was her first object to instil. Her first pupils grew up around her loving and honouring her. And as mistresses of households and mothers of families, they still found that their best friend and wisest counsellor was the gentle governess who had watched over their youth. The peasants learnt also to honour one who had worked so great a change in the character of their superiors;—the sick clung to her whose experience and knowledge rendered her as useful as a physician, whilst her gentle voice and motherlike sweetness lightened the dreariness of the dark chamber, and fell like balm upon their sufferings; mourners came to her for sympathy, which no one else knew so well how to give; little children of former pupils sprung up around her and called her blessed. Even Florestan, the wicked Prince of Monaco, acknowledged her virtues, and on more than one occasion had recourse to her knowledge of the character of his subjects, of which he himself was utterly ignorant. He recognized his sense of her services by a pension, and when the avaricious Caroline, Princess of Monaco, who had always been opposed to this unusual display of generosity, suggested on a public occasion, in hopes of drawing it back into the treasury, "that Mentone required more of Mademoiselle Lenoir than her strength would admit of, and that it would be a good thing for her if she would seek some sphere of usefulness which would be less fatiguing to her;" he was heard to reply sternly, "Caroline, it might be a good thing for Mademoiselle Lenoir if she were to give up Mentone; but it would be a bad thing indeed for Mentone if it were to lose Mademoiselle Lenoir."

Her mother died, and Mademoiselle Lenoir was left alone, yet not alone even in this world, for her former pupils clung around her like daughters, and when two years ago, illness came upon her, with sufferings which death alone can terminate, three of them, who knew the distress it would be to her if her work should fall to the ground, voluntarily undertook to keep up her school in her name, and in the room adjoining her sick chamber, her teaching still continues through their instrumentality. For two hours only in the afternoon, an interval of the most terrible suffering, is Mademoiselle Lenoir still able to see people, or occupy herself as before, and then she sometimes still has the classes to her bedside, sometimes gives advice to their teachers, sometimes admits the poor, and occasionally receives visitors. Her pension ceased at the annexation, and she was left in a state of the greatest poverty, but she has rooms in the house of General Partouneaux, the father of one of her earliest pupils, and he and his children visit her daily, and lavish the same care upon her which they would bestow upon one of their own family. When I saw her she was half sitting up in her bed, supported by pillows, her face occasionally convulsed with pain, but yet bearing an expression of the most inexpressible sweetness, cheerfulness, and resignation. When young she must have been very beautiful, and her manner is still so winning, that it is easy to understand how she has gained the influence which has made her so remarkable. Her room is full of prints and photographs, memorials of her former pupils and friends, and has a very cheerful appearance; but that which really makes you forget you are in a sick chamber, when you are with Mademoiselle Lenoir, is the inward joy and peace which beams from her eyes, and which no suffering or trial can destroy; and to her the Mentonese apply with truth their ancient proverb, "On camin ben, non mai long," "to the one who walks well, the way is never long."

THE OLD HISTORY OF THE PRINCIPALITY.

The History of Mentone is in fact that of Monaco, with which it has been linked in almost all the varied vicissitudes of its fortune, and the history of Monaco is scarcely more than that of the Grimaldi family, who have been its rulers, and whose good and bad qualities have been like a thermometer of the prosperity of the State, ever since it sprang into existence.

Until towards the commencement of the 13th century Monaco was only a deserted rock, at the foot of which, ships, coasting along the shores of Liguria and Provence, were wont to seek a refuge from the storm.

According to Dionysius of Halicarnassus, and other writers, Hercules built a temple to his own honour on this spot, after a victory over the ancient Ligurian inhabitants of the territory; ("Monœci similiter arcem et portum ad perennem sui memoriam consecravit,") which temple was served by a single priest, a hermit, a monk, (Monachus), whence some derive the name. Others believe that the name was due to the Phocians, who gave this temple the distinctive title of μονος οικος.

Long before the city of Monaco existed, the ancient Portus Herculis at its foot was known and valued. Here Augustus Cæsar embarked for Genoa, on his way to Rome, after having set up his victorious trophies at La Turbia.

"Aggeribus socer Alpinis atque arce Monœci descendens."

The neighbourhood of the Port became the scene of the combats between Otho and Vitellius, and there Fabius Valens, a general of Vitellius, landed the troops intended for the support of Marius Maturius, against a Gallic rebellion. In 286 the emperor Maximin returned by this way from his expedition against the Bogandes, a fact recorded by Claudius in the words, "Tu modo Galliæ oppida illustraveras; jam summas arces Monœci Herculis præteribas."

The scattered Ligurian village, which occupied these shores, were constantly pillaged and destroyed by the Saracens, who in 814 took possession of the heights of Esa, Turbia, and St. Agnese, whence they descended from their mountain castles to ravage the neighbourhood, the Portus Monœci itself falling entirely into their hands, and lying utterly waste during the 8th, 9th, and 10th centuries. At length among the Christian champions who appeared to do battle in their behalf, was a noble knight of Genoa, called Giballino Grimaldi, who after a great victory over the Saracens, was welcomed as a deliverer by the inhabitants, and received the lands along this beautiful gulf, as the reward of his valour. This was the beginning of the Grimaldi rule, and the first cause of the Genoese power in Monaco. All the land of the Ligurian Riviera, from Monaco to Porto Venere, was afterwards granted in fief to the Genoese by the emperor Frederick 1st; a grant which was recognised by their neighbour Count Raymond, of Provence, in a charter which gave them "Podium et montem Monaci, cum suis pertinenciis ad incastellandum." This cession was again renewed by the emperor Henry IV, on condition that the Genoese would build a castle at Monaco, for the better defence of the Christians against the Saracens.

Hitherto no building had occupied the heights of Monaco,

except a chapel, which had been built on the site of the ancient temple in 1078, by two inhabitants of La Turbia; but in consequence of this, on the 6th of June, 1191, three galleys from Genoa, containing a number of noble Genoese citizens, with one Fulco di Castello at their head, and followed by galleys laden with timber, iron, and other materials for building, disembarked at Monaco, when having defined their rights, in the presence of the imperial commissioners, by making the circuit of the desolate rock with olive boughs, they built a fortress, with four towers and circular walls, around which a new town soon began to spring up. The cession of Monaco to Genoa was ratified by the emperor Frederick II, on condition that its fortifications should be always at the service of the empire.

From 1270 to 1340, Monaco, an almost impregnable citadel, served as a refuge to the Guelfs and Ghibelines alternately, the former being represented by the Grimaldis, the latter by the Spinolas. Each party twice besieged the other within its walls, and each was twice supplanted by its opponents. On the Christmas Eve, however, of 1306, while all the inhabitants were celebrating the solemn midnight-mass, Charles Grimaldi, contrived to enter Monaco disguised as a monk, and having cut the throats of the sentinels, to let in his accomplices. From this period, with the exception of eleven years (1327—1338) the place remained in the hands of the Grimaldis, of whom Rabella Grimaldi bought a formal investment of his rights from Genoa, for 1200 gold florins.

In 1346, Charles (Grimaldi) 1st, bought part of Mentone from Emmanuel Vento of Genoa, and Roccabruna from Guiglielmo Lascaris, Count of Ventimiglia, for 16,000 florins, to which his title of Prince was recognized in 1353. The rest of Mentone was bought by another branch of the

Grimaldi family. In 1357, the Genoese, jealous of its rising importance, besieged Monaco by sea and land, and obliged it to surrender, but the exile of the Grimaldis on this occasion only lasted for a few months.

It may not be uninteresting to give a list of the earlier Princes of Monaco, merely noting the principal events of each reign.

1346. *Charles 1st.* First recognized Prince of Monaco, who was besieged by Genoa, and took refuge at Nice, whence he soon returned in triumph.

1363. *Regnier.* A brave warrior mixed up in papal politics. He first took part with Urban VI, and seized the anti-papal cardinals on their way to Avignon, as they passed through Mentone; but afterwards he changed his politics, and did equal service to the anti-Pope Clement VII. Monaco was seized and taken during his reign by Jean Grimaldi, Baron de Beuil, and his brother Louis, but not content with this conquest, they attacked Ventimiglia also, where they were both taken prisoners, and Monaco was restored to Regnier by the Genoese in 1401. Regnier was Prince of Monaco alone; his brother Charles inherited Mentone, with the title of Conseigneur.

1407. *Ambroise.*

1424. *Jean I.* As Genoa had fallen into the hands of the Viscontis, this prince, with the Conseigneur of Mentone and Roccabruna, found it prudent to espouse their cause. As a reward he received the command of the Genoese fleet, with the title of Admiral, in which capacity he gained a great victory over the Venetians, when 28 galleys and 42 transport vessels were taken, and 3000 men were killed. Returning to Genoa covered with glory, he received the sister of Doge Thomaso Frêgosa in marriage. On the expulsion of the Milanese, Jean Grimaldi was so afraid that the Genoese, in order the better to strengthen their power, might take part of his dominions away from him, that he offered the suzerainty of his outlying possessions of Roccabruna and the half of Mentone, to Louis, Duke of Savoy, to whom he did homage in 1448. From this time the Grimaldis continually did homage to the Dukes of Savoy, for their domain of Mentone and Roccabruna, presenting themselves before them, bare-headed, without boots or spurs, and receiving again the investiture of their lands as fiefs of Savoy, by the outward sign of a sword, and a kiss on the mouth, according to ancient custom. This fact was alleged as a reason for the late revolution of 1849, when Mentone and Roccabruna deserted from the government of the Princes of Monaco, and placed themselves under the protection of the King of Sardinia, declaring that they only appealed to their true Sovereign, from his provincial governor.

1454. *Catalan.*

1457. *Lambert.* This prince received Ventimiglia as the reward of services rendered to Francesco Sforza, the new Lord of Milan. But after his death, refusing allegiance to his successor Galeazzo, he was besieged in Monaco by the Duke of Savoy, ally of Genoa; but after two months blockade, agreed to the terms of a capitulation, which resulted in peace. Lambert bought from his cousins, Honorius and Luca Grimaldi, the rights which they retained over Mentone, and thus re-united all that had belonged to the Monaco Grimaldis before 1346, when the territory was divided on the death of Charles I.

1493. *Jean II.* This prince was made lieutenant of the Riviera, by Charles VIII of France, whose cause he espoused. He was murdered by his brother Lucien in 1505.

1505. *Lucien.* During the government of this prince, Genoa shook off the yoke of France, which caused many of its principal families to take flight and seek a refuge in Monaco. This led to a blockade of the town by the Genoese, which lasted five months, at the end of which time, aided by the troops of the Duke of Savoy, who occupied the heights of La Turbia, Lucien was able to make such a successful resistance, that the Genoese raised the siege. Emboldened by this triumph, Monaco shook off the yoke of the Republic. In 1515 Lucien bought from Anne de Lascaris, Countess of Villars, the feudal rights which her family still retained over Mentone, and died in 1523, murdered by his nephew Bartholomew Doria, of Dolceaqua, in the palace of Monaco.

1523. *Honorius I.* Augustino Grimaldi, Bishop of Grasse, became the guardian of this prince during his minority, and in order the better to avenge himself on the murderers of his brother Lucien, he deserted Francis I. of France, and swore allegiance to the emperor Charles V., whence began the Spanish protection of Monaco. Charles V. paid the Grimaldis a visit in 1529 at Monaco, where they had already received Pope Adrian VI. in 1522. On the death of Augustino in 1532, Stefano Grimaldi succeeded to the guardianship of the prince. He restored the Church of St. Nicholas and enlarged the palace, where he received Pope Paul III. on his way to the council of Nice. Prince Honorius himself was remarkable for his bravery, wisdom, and valour.

1581. *Charles II.*, protected by Spain, was the first prince who refused to do homage to the Dukes of Savoy, for Mentone and Roccabruna, which he was consequently declared to have forfeited, after a solemn trial in 1583.

1589. *Hercules,* relying on the protection of Spain, persisted in refusing to do homage to Savoy for Mentone and Roccabruna. From this time the protection which Spain had granted to the Grimaldi family, became a yoke over their possessions. Hence the remains of the Spanish language which are still perceptible in the more remote parts of the principality. Hercules, being accused by some of the inhabitants of Monaco of dishonouring their daughters, was summarily thrown into the sea by them and drowned, in 1604.

1604. *Honorius II.* Advantage was taken by Philip III. of Spain of the minority of this prince, to introduce a fixed Spanish garrison into Monaco, but on his coming of age, he determined to shake off the Spanish yoke; and having placed Monaco under the protection of France, by a treaty with Richelieu at Peronne, he contrived to surprise the Spanish garrison by night and expel them for ever. The government of this sovereign, which lasted 58 years, was wise and paternal, and his death was the cause of universal mourning; but the foreign tyranny still continued, the only difference being that Monaco was occupied by a French instead of a Spanish garrison. Honorius was succeeded by his grandson.

1662. *Louis I.* This prince, equally remarkable for his own vices, and for the severe laws which he drew up to guard the virtue of his subjects, was made ambassador from France to Rome, where he was so ruined by his luxurious mode of living, that in order to replenish his coffers, he forced his subjects to relinquish their rights over the oil-mills which belonged to them; a usurpation of which the Princes of Monaco till very recently continued to take advantage. Louis died at Rome.

1701. *Antoine,* who in 1714, after an appeal on the

part of the Duke of Savoy to the Assembly General of Utrecht, which referred it to the Courts of France and England, was obliged to renew the homage due from the Princes of Monaco to the Dukes of Savoy, for Mentone and Roccabruna. This prince had no sons, but married his eldest daughter Louise Hippolyte Grimaldi to Jacques de Torigny, Count de Matignon, who consented to bear the arms and name of Grimaldi, and who, by the marriage contract, was appointed the successor of Antoine, contrary to the law regulating fiefs of the empire, by which women have no right of succession. Antoine was the only Prince of Monaco, except Honorius II., who devoted himself to the welfare of his people, and the only one who was really regretted by them.

1731. *Louise Hippolyte.* The Count de Matignon, entitled by his marriage contract to succeed his father-in-law, came to take possession of Monaco; but the people refused to accept him as their ruler, and conferred the sovereign title upon the Princess Louise Hippolyte. The Count yielded to this manifestation of the popular will, and retired to Paris. In consequence of the authority with which she was invested, the Princess, in 1731, did homage to Charles Emmanuel III. for the fiefs of Mentone and Roccabruna, after the manner of her ancestors, but died within the year. In her became extinct the ancient house of the Monaco Grimaldis. She was succeeded by her eldest son.

1731. *Honorius III.* of Grimaldi Matignon, who did homage to King Victor Amadeus III. for the fiefs of Mentone and Roccabruna. The marriage of this prince gave a curious example of the aristocratic bondage which preceded the French Revolution. Falling passionately in love with the beautiful Catarina de Brignole, niece of the Doge of Genoa, he demanded her hand of her father, and his proposals being favourably received, a deputy was sent to fetch the bride from Genoa to the Port of Hercules. A question, however, of etiquette which arose on her arrival, was near putting an end to every thing; and this was, whether the bride should land to meet the prince, or, whether the prince should go on board to meet the bride. As neither would yield, the Countess mother declared that she should carry her daughter back to Genoa, when after a furious discussion, she was at length induced to agree to a flying bridge being thrown from the galley to the shore, on which the prince and his fiancée both agreed to advance half-way. Honorius had two sons, Honorius IV., who married Louise d'Aumont, Duchèss of Mazarin, and Joseph, who married a daughter of the Maréchal de Choiseul.

The French Revolution, in its general overthrow of governments, did not pass over that of Monaco. Early in 1790, a deputation was sent to Honorius III., representing the grievances of the people, and demanding a municipality with popular suffrage. His only answer was to hurry back to his state, resolved to crush the new ideas in the bud, but the attitude of the people was so threatening on his arrival, that he was thankful to grant all they demanded, and to return to France as quickly as possible.

A year afterwards, imagining that the Revolution had passed over, he withdrew the concessions which fear had forced from him, and made the yoke of his absolute power weigh more heavily upon his people than ever. It was not long before the French army crossed the Var, took possession of Nice, and proclaimed the abolition of the feudal system in the possessions of the Prince of Monaco, who was thus deprived of his sovereignty. Prince Honorius III. was a man of intelligence and distinction,

THE OLD HISTORY OF THE PRINCIPALITY. 37

but of dissolute manners; a prince celebrated for his magnificence, but detested for his tyranny. He died at Paris in 1795.

Incorporated with France by a decree of the Convention of the 15th February, 1793, and comprised in the department of the Maritime Alps, the ex-principality of Monaco followed the revolutionary movement in all its phases, only remaining free from its sanguinary excesses. The people burnt Pope Pius VI. in effigy in the Piazza of Monaco; yet, only a few months later, when the vessel which bore his remains, was forced by a tempest to seek shelter in the Port of Hercules, all the town came together like one man to do him honour, and his coffin was deposited in the principal church, where funeral honours were rendered to him. A similar welcome was given 13 years later to the living Pius VII., when he passed through Mentone in 1814, on his return to Rome from exile.

When the European powers, united at Paris, were dividing the empire, which victory had given to Napoleon, the tiny principality of Monaco seemed at first to be forgotten, and likely to be restored as part of Nice to the house of Savoy, to whom all the territory of the Republic of Genoa was given up. But, by a strange exception, due, it is said, to the interested intervention of Talleyrand, a line was allowed to be inserted in the 8th article of the treaty, which declared that "the principality of Monaco should be replaced in the relations in which it existed before the 1st of January 1792."

By this unexpected exception in their favour, the house of Matignon-Grimaldi recovered the sovereignty which it had lost for twenty-one years; the article of the treaty of Peronne, which placed their State under the protection of France, being maintained by the Powers.

The new Prince *Honorius IV.* (eldest son of Honorius III.) was incapacitated from governing by illness, and his duties devolved on his brother Joseph, who was justly popular with the inhabitants. Unfortunately his rule was of short duration; the government fell into the hands of his nephew, the Duke of Valentinois, who took the name of *Honorius V.* of fatal memory.

The tranquillity of this reign and of that which followed, though unmoved by the sufferings of the people, was long and seriously disturbed by another cause, which was no less than the appearance of a rival branch of the Grimaldi family, who laid claim to the throne of Monaco, and whose rights, never wholly disproved, are still believed in by many persons.

The direct male line of Grimaldi had become extinct in the year 1748, in the person of Honoré François, Archbishop of Besançon. This personage had however before yielded his rights to his niece Louise-Hippolyte, Countess of Goyon Matignon, who was enabled by the virtues of her father Antoine, and the love and gratitude with which he had inspired his subjects, to succeed to his Sovereignty in 1731, in spite of the law which prohibited females from inheriting, if any agnats, that is to say, males descended from males of the family, were still in existence.

At the time, however, that Louise Hippolyte took possession of her sovereignty, two agnat branches of the families were still in existence, one nearly related, the issue of Gaspard Grimaldi, Marquis of Cagnes, the other more distantly, the issue of Luchetto Grimaldi, Seigneur della Pietra, who lived in the 15th century.

When Louise Hippolyte took possession, the Marquis of Cagnes was too young to contend with her in behalf of his rights, and no one could be found who was willing to act for him; afterwards he grew up too indolent to support his own cause; but on Jan. 12, 1761, one of his sons, the Marquis of Sauveur Gaspard, addressed a protestation to the court of France against what he called the usurpation of the Counts of Matignon. In 1774 he renewed this protest at Vienna before the aulic council, where his pretensions were taken into consideration.

It was placed beyond dispute that the fiefs of Monaco, Mentone, and Roccabruna, were true imperial fiefs, and consequently that Louise Hippolyte de Grimaldi, married to Count Jacques de Matignon, could not have taken possession without violating the well-known laws which regulated the succession in all fiefs of this kind. No further notice was taken at the time of the application of the Marquis Sauveur Gaspard, and 15 years later the French revolution swept away, for the time, both the dispute and the cause of it.

After the restoration, this branch of the house of Grimaldi, revived their claims. Thus on Jan. 21, 1841, before King Charles Albert could give to Prince Florestan the investiture of Mentone and Roccabruna, the Marquis Charles Philippe Auguste de Cagnes, at that time residing at Saint Marcellin in France, addressed a memorial to the Sardinian government to justify his rights of preference, and to demand the suspension of the infeudation. The king, being doubtless of opinion that this infeudation, which was only a repetition of those which had already taken place in 1716, 1733, 1775, 1812, 1816, could not injure the rights of the Marquis if they were well founded, did not think it right to yield to his request, and conferred the investiture in question upon Prince Florestan. The Marquis de Cagnes formally protested against the validity of this act, in a note which he sent on Jan. 16, 1842, to the Cabinet of Turin, but the feeling excited in his favour was of short duration, and though this branch of the house of Grimaldi have never ceased to assert their rights to the sovereignty of Monaco, the descendants of Louise Hippolyte still enjoy it.

MODERN TYRANTS AND REVOLUTIONS.

HONORIUS V. entered upon his sovereignty with a lie upon his lips, and closed it in the same manner. As he was passing through Cannes, on his return from Paris to Monaco, on March 1, 1815, his carriage was stopped by soldiers. These were the sentinels which Napoleon, on landing from Elba, had posted on the road to Italy. On being led into the presence of the Emperor, Honorius received from his former master an invitation to accompany him to Paris; he refused, promising nevertheless to await the commands of the Emperor in his own State, and then he continued his journey. On his arrival at Nice he forgot his promise, and hastened to inform the government that Napoleon had landed in Provence. The government immediately provided for the security of the frontier, and embarked the English troops which were at Nice for the Port of Hercules. They were relieved in the month of June by an Anglo-Italian regiment in the pay of England, who occupied Monaco until the second treaty of Paris.

By this treaty of Nov. 20, 1815, Monaco was removed from the protection which France had exercised over it for 173 years, the protective right being restored to Sardinia, by whose states the principality was surrounded. In consequence, King Victor Emmanuel I. placed a Sardinian garrison in the fortress of Monaco, and received (Nov. 30,

1816) the homage of the Prince for his domains of Mentone and Roccabruna: a final proof that these were only fiefs received from the house of Savoy, and subject to its sovereign jurisdiction.

The Revolution had deprived the Princes of Monaco of the greater part of their feudal property: at least that which remained was insufficient for their habits of princely life, and their tastes of hereditary luxury; and the little State to which they returned was unable to restore their former splendour; especially in the impoverished condition, caused by the barrier of custom houses, which now separated it from France. The pacific dispositions of the people made them willing to make any necessary sacrifice in behalf of their princes, yet this generosity of feeling was little reciprocated.

The former princes, who were both rich and generous, only levied light customs, of which the produce was used in the public expenses, for the profit of the country, while their presence in the midst of their people was a benefit, and a just subject of rejoicing. But the new Sovereigns, ruined by the Revolution, demanded the reparation of their losses, and that the people, while replenishing their treasuries, should satisfy their thirst for luxury. The customs rose to nearly 90,000 francs, including what came from the tobacco manufactory, and the Port of Monaco. The taxes, constantly increased and multiplied, speedily rose to 300,000 francs.

Honorius V. being resolved to revive all the abuses of the old system, for his own profit, with all the oppressions of feudal power, entered upon his principality, with the idea that it was his private property, and that its inhabitants were his serfs. He considered that goods and people alike belonged to him in this land, where his ancestors had reigned; the restoration must give him back that which the revolution had taken away, if not, he would take it back for himself. Thus he lived, as if he was only acting in the simplest, most legitimate way possible, during the whole twenty-five years of his reign, gorging himself with the public substance, but keeping at a distance from the country he was ruining. During this time Honorius V. only made short sojourns of a few days each among his unhappy people, and then returned to France, with all the riches he could collect.

In Paris, Honorius hoped to be beyond the reach of murmurs, and his people were forbidden under severe penalties to address any petition to him, however oppressive their yoke might be. Meanwhile Monaco was systematically plundered; the property of the communes, hospitals, and churches, and the product of the customs, being alike confiscated to the Prince. This was followed by the sequestration of the public revenues, even to the contents of the poor boxes and collections made in churches. The four mills of the commune, which the old princes and the French government had equally respected, were the next objects seized upon, and the inhabitants were forced to shut up their own mills, without obtaining the least compensation, and commanded to grind their olives in the mills of the Prince, under the severest penalties. Every thing was heavily taxed, both on entering the State, and leaving it; oranges, lemons, grapes, essences, oil, in fact the whole produce of the country; and since France and Sardinia both taxed their importation, the exportation-tax almost reduced their value to nothing.

Not content with levying a tribute upon commerce, Honorius soon seized the monopoly of it. He established at Monaco, a manufactory of linen cloth of every description, cloth which was not so good, and much dearer than that elsewhere, yet none of his subjects were allowed to buy from any other than himself; and the boatmen and fishermen of Monaco, especially, were forced to procure all the sails of their vessels from the Prince's manufactory. The monopoly of gunpowder, pipes, cards, ammunition of every kind, and straw hats, were the next things seized upon. The shambles followed, and then, what was far more trying to his subjects, pollenta, which formed almost the entire sustenance of the lower orders.

Honorius however was still in want of money, so he proceeded to make himself at once the only farmer, miller and baker of his country; in a word, to seize the monopoly of "Cereales." For this purpose he brought from Paris a man who had been an army contractor, to whom he committed the monopoly of the corn, flour and bread of the whole principality, on condition of sharing the profits himself, forbidding his subjects to buy anywhere else. Wanting mills for his purpose, he seized the oil mills of his subjects, paying an indemnity which was a mere mockery, and converting them into flour mills; while in order to construct a road to lead to them, he levied an enormous highway rate, which if any proprietor was unable to pay, his neighbour was obliged to pay for him. From this time all strangers passing through Monaco, as well as the inhabitants, were forced to eat the same bread, which was sold at an exorbitant price, though made from refuse flour, bought at a nominal price in the markets of Marseilles and Genoa, and often so bad as to be quite unwholesome.

Whenever the municipal police of Genoa prohibited the sale of some damaged corn, the prince's contractor immediately bought it up, declaring that it was only too good for the people of Monaco. If any good corn was by chance found in the warehouses at Monaco, it was immediately *exported to be re-sold,* and worse grain bought in its place. The price of this horrible bread rose till it became double than in any other place; then the people addressed a petition to their prince. His only answer was a threat of severe punishment, and the declaration that he would rule them with a rod of iron, "*qu'il ferait peser sur eux un bras de fer.*"

Any attempts of the unhappy inhabitants to obtain bread from Nice, were frustrated by the cordon of surveillance drawn around the principality, and all such signs of rebellion were immediately punished. Even travellers, passing through Monaco, were forced to give up any provisions they might have, on arriving at the frontiers, and the Sardinian workman on crossing the boundary was not allowed to bring with him even his dinner of the day. If the owner of any boat from a strange port, on entering the Port of Monaco, had left uneaten any part of the loaves of bread with which his vessel was furnished on leaving home, he was taught by the confiscation of his vessel and a fine of 500 francs to calculate better another time.

The surveillance of the police did not end out of doors. Private families were watched, private houses entered, and if the consumption of bread in every house was not equal to that which was expected, its inmates were suspected of obtaining contraband food, and were liable to be arrested.

In order still further to fill up the deficiencies in his treasury, caused by the Revolution, the Prince forced those who had acquired any of the lands which had belonged to his ancestors, to give them up without any indemnity. No one in the principality was allowed to export wood, except the prince himself, and no one was ever allowed to cut down a bough from one of their own olive trees, unless the stroke were authorized by the government, and given in the presence of the officials. No one was allowed to sell their own crops, except at a price fixed by the police, and then the purchaser, instead of paying the sum to the proprietor, was obliged to bring his money to a receiver-general established by the prince, who exacted one per cent. on the sale. In a short time no one was allowed to till their own land or water it, or to prune their own trees, without the permission of the police; and at last no one was permitted to leave their house after 10 o'clock at night, without being furnished with a lanthorn, which was also a pretext for a fine. The taxes became at length too absurd for belief. The birth or death of an animal had to be entered in the public register on the same day, on payment of a fine, and was of course taxed. The tax on the birth of a lamb was 25 centimes.

As petitions or complaints to the Prince were more heavily taxed than any thing else, the police had all their own way, and could oppress the people in any manner they pleased.

The difficulties occasioned by the passport, which every one was obliged to have in order to cross the frontier, made attempts to escape from this oppressed land nearly impossible; and as the State was only two leagues in width, an expenditure of three francs was often necessary, even for an ordinary walk.

Out of a population of 6,500 inhabitants, Honorius contrived to extract an income of 350,000 francs a-year, of which 80,000 served to pay the guards and officials of the government, and the rest was squandered by the Prince himself in France, at a distance of 300 leagues from his unhappy people. For twenty-one years Honorius's tyranny continued, and then with one voice his people gave thanks to God for his death. On the right of the altar, in the last chapel of the parish church at Monaco, is his grave; still an object of abhorrence to his subjects, and bearing the inscription on its surface, which records the falsehood his dying lips commanded to be placed there, "Ci git qui voulut le bien."

Honorius V. left the succession to his brother *Florestan Roger Louis de Grimaldi*, married in 1816 to Marie Louise Caroline Gilbert, of Metz, a lady who became at once the actual Sovereign, though her husband was the nominal one, and whose mis-government was the cause of the Revolution which ensued.

Florestan himself was a mere nonentity, without either vices or virtues: utterly unequal to the position to which he was called, he succumbed at once to the imperious character of his wife, from whom he seldom ventured to differ. "He did no wrong himself; nevertheless he allowed others to do it in his name."

Still the accession of Florestan inspired fresh hopes. On his first arrival at Mentone, the people suddenly surrounded his carriage, whilst he was visiting the Governor, and unharnessing the horses, awaited his exit, crying out with one voice, "A bas l'Exclusive! A bas les Monopoles." The Prince overwhelmed with terror, yielded on the spot to this imperious demand, and promised to abolish all the monopolies, especially that of food, and a few days after, the liberty of "Cereales" was actually proclaimed, and the unwholesome bread disappeared, to the advantage both of the health and fortunes of the people. But still the Prince, or rather the Princess, retained the monopoly for the grinding of corn.

People soon found out, that what the government let go with one hand, they seized with the other. The duties on the export of fruits had been so heavy, that the proprietors had been driven to cut down their trees, the merchants to shut up their warehouses, the ship-owners to sink their vessels. These duties were lowered, but only sufficiently to prevent driving the inhabitants to actual despair, and this was the sole concession which the cupidity of the new government allowed them to make. For the rest, there were the same extortions, and the same despotic rule.

The void in the treasury was filled up by expedients, which maintained the amount of the annual civil list at 320,000 francs. Since the State contained only 6,500 inhabitants, this was a taxation of more than 50 francs a-head. Since 1815 more than six millions had been extracted from the State, and expended at Paris, not one centime having been allowed to benefit the country whence it came.

By the treaties of 1815 the Prince of Monaco was bound to give to his principality the same laws which were in force in Sardinia, and the people presented a humble petition to Florestan, begging that he would carry out the conditions of those treaties. To this address he harshly replied, "Je ne veux rien entendre, je suis ici pour gouverner moi-même. Je n'ai besoin de conseil de personne."

Hardly repressing his indignation at such an answer, one of the deputation added, " Toujours est il, prince, que nous sommes heureux, que votre Altesse ait entendu l'expression de nos voeux et de nos besoins." " Vos besoins, je les connais," answered the Prince, cooly turning his back upon the deputation. Henceforward there was nothing left for the people, but patient submission, and the hope of brighter days.

The Prince's visits to Monaco became more and more rare, and when he did appear, it was only to lay some new burden upon his oppressed subjects.

When the Italian crisis came in 1847, the Prince was in Paris, whence the call of duty urged him to hasten immediately to his principality, yet he dared not face his unhappy subjects, or quit Paris, for a voice from the pontifical throne had already announced to Italy that the hour for its emancipation was arrived, and that Pius IX. had begun to grant reforms in Rome.

The principality of Monaco, filled with joy at the thought of coming freedom, turned hopefully towards Charles Albert as its liberator. His birthday, 4th Nov. 1847, was memorable in the history of Mentone, for on that day its streets resounded with cries of "Viva Pio Nono, Viva il Re di Sardaigno." This first energetic demonstration was followed up three days afterwards by a procession of the whole population of the town, headed by the dignitaries of the church and the municipal authorities, to the Governor's house, begging him to present their former petition to the Prince of Monaco, that they might henceforward be governed by the same laws and institutions which were in operation in the Sardinian territory. The Governor promised to transmit this petition to the Prince, and second it with his influence. On the 16th a despatch arrived from Paris, in which the Prince promised the desired reforms; but a rumour gaining ground that a second and confidential despatch had come to the government, annulling the first, and ordering the arrest of all malcontents, caused the people, now in the greatest excitement, to surround the government house, demanding to hear the promises of the Prince ratified by his own lips.

At length, Florestan, dreading a revolt, decided on leaving Paris, and returning to his State; but, on arriving at Monaco, instead of courageously meeting his subjects, he shut himself up in his palace, and forbade the authorities and people of Mentone to present themselves before him. The people of Roccabruna, equally desirous of reform, were equally forbidden access; and when a month later the deputies of the people, ventured to present an address to the Prince, they were repulsed with violence. This brought public frenzy to a climax: crowds traversed the town with flags flying, singing Italian hymns to Liberty, their complaints mingling with appeals to the honoured name of Charles Albert.

The Prince, for a moment, seemed inclined to yield, and his son, the Duke of Valentinois, was commissioned to enter into a negotiation with the people, but this was soon discovered to be merely a new deception; and the agitation began again by the shipowners being summoned, and reproached by the Prince with being subservient to the rich, to which these brave men replied, "Nous ne faisons qu' un; nos interets et nos vœux sont communs, et nous sommes unis, voyez vous, comme les cinque doigts de la main. C'a été toujours ainsi, et sera toujours." The irritation of the Prince at this reply, led to the arrest of several of his most influential subjects, even the aged Curé of Mentone being denounced as a factious person, and sent to be examined by the Bishop of Nice, from whom he returned with praises and wishes for "a better fortune."

At length, all attempts having failed to induce the Prince to act in a straightforward manner, wearied with concessions which always proved delusive, the people of

Mentone and Roccabruna, after 33 years of patient submission, finally threw off the yoke of Monaco, and on the 2nd of March, 1848, unfurled the flag of Italy, and proclaimed themselves "Free towns under the protection of Sardinia." Thus was brought about a revolution, which though perhaps the smallest, was certainly the most unanimous, which has ever occurred in history. The first care of the provisional government, consisting of 100 inhabitants of the liberated cities, was to send an explanation of what had happened to the courts of France and Sardinia, with a request that their consuls would respect the flag of Italy, which had been adopted by Mentone and Roccabruna. A favorable answer was returned at once from Turin, and after some further explanation, M. Lamartine, then Minister of foreign affairs in France, also recognized their independence. The revolution thus became a "fait accompli," and was celebrated by a Te Deum, which was sung publicly in the parish church of Mentone.

Monaco alone of all his former dominions, was now left to the Prince, who in vain tried to beguile the rest of his subjects back to their allegiance.

The earnest desire of the two free towns was to be united to Piedmont; a wish so unanimous, that during the five days appointed for taking votes on this subject, not one contrary vote was registered. A deputation was sent to Turin, to present the petition to Charles Albert, who received it favourably; and although the calumnies spread by the partizans of the Prince of Monaco, induced the French to interfere, alleging that votes had been bought, and that women and children had signed the petition, they were soon convinced of the injustice of the accusation, and the opposition was withdrawn. The Chamber of Deputies at Turin, decreed that Mentone and Roccabruna should be governed as the other states of the kingdom, and should form an integral part of them. A royal commissioner was sent to organize the two communes, and several of the Sardinian laws were published and put in force. Meantime, the news of the annexation was hailed with the utmost joy, and its influence soon changed the whole aspect of the country. Schools, hospitals, and fountains, were reopened and repaired, agriculture began once more to flourish, and commerce to be profitable.

The only question now raised was as to the amount of the indemnity which should be paid by the towns to their former rulers. "Propose to the Prince a suitable indemnity," was the demand of the French Cabinet to that of Turin, "and if he does not act reasonably, we will abandon his cause." Consequently, Florestan knew that if he refused to listen to the negotiation all would be lost. Every proposition, however, made by Sardinia, as to an annual rent to be paid for Mentone and Roccabruna, or as to the purchase of Monaco itself, was rejected by the Prince, and at length he mentioned conditions, to which it was impossible to accede. On Septr. 22nd, 1852, a deputation sent to Louis Napoleon, then President of the French Republic, met with promises of sympathy and help, and though in the next two years, the question of the annexation of the free towns to Sardinia was almost forgotten, in the great events which followed; France no longer made any opposition to it.

It was desired by the Sardinian government that Monaco itself should be included in the annexation, but this project the Duke of Valentinois was determined to baffle. He had formed a plan for establishing an international bank at Monaco, as a centre for all the provincial commerce of the Mediterranean; and being of determined and enterprising character, he resolved to make a last effort to recover his lost patrimony, and for this purpose made overtures to all the great powers to assist him, even to Austria, the hereditary enemy of his country; but the attention of these powers was too fully engrossed by the political changes then agitating Europe to allow of their espousing his cause.

Three years of peace and prosperity had passed, when, despairing of foreign assistance, the Duke of Valentinois once more made an attempt to repossess himself of Mentone. On the 6th of April, 1854, at 6 o'clock in the morning, he arrived at the Hotel de Turin, in a gilt carriage decorated with the royal arms of Monaco, wearing the splendid uniform of the principality, with the emblems of the various orders to which he belonged, and accompanied by two of his principal officers. Here three or four persons meeting him raised the cry of "Vive le Prince," which brought out about thirty men and women, who, taking the horses from the carriage, drew it through the principal street, carrying before it a flag bearing the arms of the Grimaldi family. The alarm had however been given, and on the appearance of the National guard, these few adherents of royalty fled in consternation, leaving him to the anger of the crowd. The Duke descended from his carriage, sword in hand, and such was the exasperation of the people, that he would probably have paid for his temerity by his life, had not the Quarter-master of the Carabineers, with two of his men, arrived in time to rescue him; the Duke then begged to be taken to a place of safety, and was conducted to the barracks. The National Guard and people of Roccabruna hearing of the Duke's arrival, hastened in arms to help the Mentonese. The authorities of Nice being informed of what was going on at Mentone, sent M. de la Marmora, the Commander of the Carabineers, and M.

Faraldo, to investigate the affair, and after making the fullest enquiries, both from the people and the Duke himself, they deemed it best, for the safety of the latter, to take him to Nice, and retain him in the Castle of Villa Franca, till the Sardinian government had been informed of his attempt to regain the town.

After this time, Mentone and Roccabruna led a peaceful and free existence for nine years, under the Sardinian protectorate, during which time, both places increased annually in wealth and prosperity. The discovery of Mentone by the English, as a warm and healthful winter residence, brought each year an increasing number of strangers, many of whom have bought land, and built beautiful villas in the neighbourhood. The new road to Sospello and Turin offered an outlet to commerce and native productions, and the freedom from taxes and customs, and consequent increase of profit upon labour, gave an additional stimulus to the native industry.

In 1860 the war in Piedmont led to the cession of Nice to France. It was then left to the people of Mentone and Roccabruna, to choose whether they would remain Italian, or become French; whether they would oppose the annexation to France, or vote for it; and they chose the latter. How far they were led to this step, by the false impression that a union with France would facilitate the exportation of their oranges and lemons; how far they were biassed by their syndic, who had married a French wife, and whose partialities have never been disguised, although he was appointed by the Sardinian government; how far they were influenced by the Partouneaux family, which have long been resident among them, must remain unknown, but it is certain that the people repent bitterly now of what they have done, and repent too late. The renewal of taxation and conscription are among the troubles they have brought back upon themselves.

"We were free, but we took our liberty and trampled it under our feet," is now the repentant cry of many a poor Mentonese.

When Sardinia had given up her claims upon Mentone and Roccabruna, and when the two Communes had given themselves away, it still remained for France to satisfy the claims of their ancient ruler, the Prince of Monaco, who had never yet recognized them as belonging to any other than himself, though they had so long ceased to pay him taxes, or shew deference to his authority. This was done (February 1861) by purchasing his claim upon his unprofitable dominions for £600,000, for which sum he consented to give up everything, except the rock of Monaco itself, with its huge neglected palace, and the title of his ancestors. Even Monaco is now liable to French conscription and taxation, so that the authority of the Prince is reduced to little more than that of a syndic in his own metropolis.

SANTA DEVOTA AND MONACO.

We have at last penetrated to the head quarters of this history, and been in a carriage to Monaco, which would have been worth even ten times the jolting we underwent to get there; though it is indeed, as the natives say, "une vraie penitence." The road to Monaco follows that to Nice above the Cape St. Martin, till it turns down below Roccabruna, which clings to the hill-side amid its broken crags. From this point Monaco is in sight the whole way, her white walls gleaming on an almost isolated rock, but a succession of little valleys with steep ascents and descents have to be traversed in order to reach it. Nothing can be more beautiful than the variety of greens in these valleys, the blue green of the gigantic euphorbias, which fringe the rocks by the wayside; the grey green of the olives; the dark green of the old gnarled coruba trees; and the yellow green of the canes and the vineyards, especially in autumn. Each valley has its torrent, crossed sometimes by a high bridge, sometimes only by open arches, which look like a bridge from below, but really only form a parapet to the road, beneath which the water rushes, while travellers splash through the stream, or cross the stepping stones under their protection. The walls are tufted with lovely maidenhair fern, which the natives call Erba della Fontana (fountain grass) and drink in tea.

A little ruined edifice on the right of the way, is the

"Chapelle du Bon Voyage," which before the Revolution was one of the most celebrated places of pilgrimage on the coast. Then everyone in the neighbourhood who was going a journey came hither to pray; and people would even come from twenty leagues distance to ask a blessing at the Bon Voyage before sailing for foreign parts. The people of Monaco still pray before the ruins when starting for a journey.

The summit of the ascent beyond this is crowned by a curious rock, known as "the monk," a gigantic, natural figure, sitting on the mountain side with its head buried in its cowl. Beyond this is seen "the nun," sitting higher up on the edge of the cliff.

Passing the tiny custom house of Monaco, one arrives at Veilles, a village perched on a ledge of the tufa rock, over which a mill-stream dashes, amid a luxuriant profusion of aloes, cactus, and hanging creepers. This was the "Vigiliæ" of Augustus, surrounded in his time by military outposts. A large stone found here and now transported to the palace at Monaco, bears the inscription,

JUL CAESAR
AUGUSTUS IMP $\overline{\text{X}}$
TRIBUNITIA
POTESTATE $\overline{\text{X}}$
DCI

Two torrents beyond this, is a ravine, rendered memorable as the place where a number of French soldiers were assassinated by the Barbets, a band of mountaineers who, under pretext of loyalty, gave themselves up to cruelty and rapine, during the invasion of 1792.

At the entrance of the valley of Gaumates, the last

before reaching Monaco, the rocks which form its northern barrier divide to let a small mountain torrent issue forth to join the sea. Above, the chasm is spanned by a lofty yellow arch, while beneath, nestling in the ravine by the side of the streamlet, is a picturesque little chapel, painted on the outside with coats of arms, and approached from the road by a short avenue of venerable ilex trees. It is a tempting subject for an artist, and the little chapel, which now contains nothing but a few mouldy pictures and rusty chandeliers, is interesting as being all that remains to mark the once famous shrine and monastery of Sta. Devota. This saint was a christian virgin of Corsica, martyred with cruel tortures, in the reign of Diocletian, by the Roman governor of that island. According to the Lerins Chronicles, "In order that she might not be buried by the Christians, this barbarian ordered her body to be reduced to ashes, but the priest Bevenato and the deacon Apollinaris, being warned in a vision to remove the body of the saint from the island, came by night, embarked it, and set sail with a sailor named Gratien, intending to land on the coast of Africa. Their efforts were in vain, and all night long they were driven back by a south wind, which carried them towards the coast of Liguria. The following morning, while the sailor was asleep, the saint appeared to him in a dream, and told him to continue his course with joy, and to observe that which should come out of her mouth, which would be a sign to let him know where she would wish to be buried. In truth, the pilot, on awaking, saw, as well as his two companions, a white dove issue from the mouth of the saint, and take the direction of Monaco. They followed it with their eyes, till it rested in the valley called Gaumates, situated on the east of the city. There she was buried, and there an oratory was afterwards built to her, with a monastery attached to it, under the dependance of the monastery of St. Pons." Another legend describes that the vessel bearing the remains of the saint was wrecked off Monaco, and that only one fragment of it drifted into the Port of Hercules, bearing the dead body of a beautiful maiden lashed upon it, and an inscription telling that it was that of Devota, the Corsican Virgin and Martyr.

The festival of Sta. Devota (January 27) was formerly celebrated at Gaumates, with great splendour; pilgrimages were made to the chapel, and the ancient money of the country bore her effigy, but the devotion to her shrine, has long since gone out of fashion; fewer and fewer pilgrims came, and at last, to avoid starvation, the monks of Gaumates fled to the superior monastery of St. Pons, and left their own little convent to ruin. Among the privileges which they preserved to the last, was the right possessed by the Prior and one other of their number, chosen by the prince, to read Vespers on the eve of their saint, and high mass on her fête, in the parish church of Monaco, and also of *opening the ball* which celebrated the same occasion, a privilege of which these ecclesiastical dignitaries never failed to avail themselves. At the same time, the monks presented some artichokes to the prince in token of homage, and enjoyed his hospitality for three days, at the end of which time they were dismissed with tokens of his liberality.

Sta. Devota is at the entrance of the once famous Port of Hercules, frequently mentioned by classical authors, and formerly the terror of the rich merchants of Genoa, from the number of pirates and corsairs, to whom it was a shelter and a home. Now, it is almost filled up by long neglect, and gives refuge to nothing, but the little steamer which brings people hither three times a week from Nice, and a few fishing-boats, whose tall white sails are mirrored in its still waters, as they nestle under the rocky edge of the hill. Smaller boats are constantly employed in fishing for the "Frutte di Mare," which abound in the bay, and looking much like chestnuts, are divided and eaten in the same manner. From this little port many French emigrants made their escape in the reign of terror, gaining the large foreign vessels, which were lying off Monaco, in small fishing-boats. Among them, say the natives, was a young Englishman who had been married in France, and had lived there. He arrived with a chest of gold, so heavy that it required four men to move it, and after he embarked, he never was heard of again; it is supposed he was murdered for the sake of that chest. On the opposite side of the bay, are a long row of unfinished baths, which might have proved a great source of attraction to Monaco, but which, like a large casino whose stones still litter the neighbouring olive wood, and many other things here, are still unfinished for want of money. They stand in a state of melancholy ruin, and are only an eye-sore to the pleasant little Hotel des Etrangers which is close beside them, and whose garden is worth entering for the sake of admiring its tall and beautiful palm tree.

Two roads lead up from hence into the town; the upper going straight up into the court of the palace through the Porte St. Antoine; the lower leading through the Porte Neuve into the Boschetto, otherwise called the "Promenade St. Martin." Here it is like being launched at once into the tropics; the terraces are carpeted with aloes, some of which raise their golden stems crowned by masses of flower, as high as the tops of the cypresses, which are mingled with them. The wild luxuriance of cactus and plants of the same tribe, not content with covering the heights, overrun the walls and clothe the precipitous cliffs down to the very edge of the sea. Splendid geraniums fringe the road and mingle in huge masses with purple stocks, and tall star-flowered asphodel, while here and there a palm tree raises its umbrella of delicate foliage into the blue sky. Below, on two sides, is the sea, with its varied outline of headlands, behind is the deserted monastery of the Visitazione, now turned into a barrack, and the white houses of the town. The number of ladies sitting out upon the terraces, and the well-dressed children playing about, give the promenade a most animated appearance. Indeed the fact of this paradise having been so long rendered the abode of misery by the wickedness of its government reminds one of a story of the Spaniard, who declared that the only reason why the Madonna had not blest his country with a good government, as well as all other benefits, was, because she was afraid that if she did, Spain would become so delightful and alluring, that she should not be able to keep any of the angels in heaven.

There is an air of great comfort about the town, which is said to be partly owing to the fact that the dowager princess generally makes it her residence for six months in the year, while the prince following the example of his predecessors, still prefers spending his large fortune in Paris, and lives altogether in France. The roads are excellent, and even the streets are covered with fine gravel instead of a rough pavement, and have an unusual appearance of cleanliness. The houses are now almost all modernized; formerly by a local custom all the windows were arched and divided into two parts, with a cross in the centre, and a stone ledge beneath, from which fishing nets or clothes were hung out to dry. Many of these houses were in existence only fifteen years ago. The church of Sta. Barbara is large and handsome, and possesses a portico which is said to be a fragment of a Roman temple. There is a tablet here commemorating the funeral ceremonies which were bestowed upon Pius VI. in this church, when, a few months after he had been burnt in effigy by the republican populace, shipwreck drove his dead body upon their shores. The last chapel on the right contains the graves and monumental tablets of the later Princes of Monaco, among which is the lying inscription to the hated Honorius V. Some of the pictures are old and curious.

The Gambling-house, which, to their disgrace, the Princes have introduced into their state, has a pretty garden with a fine palm tree.

The Piazza (which contains an excellent hotel, de Russie) is closed on the north by the palace, an immense building, which has been added to or altered in almost every successive reign, each prince bringing his own taste and his own prejudices to bear upon the work. It would be difficult to say what was its exact appearance before the year 1538, which was the date of its enlargement and restoration. But it is probable, nevertheless, that all the eastern side, and the principal part of the existing facade, which at that time extended to the ramparts, are little changed, and go back to an earlier period, perhaps nearly to the time of the foundation of the building. The western part seems to belong almost entirely to the time of the Spanish government. As for that on the north, it is possible that it may have undergone some important modifications, but it is certain that it existed, with a chapel in its centre, under the reign of Lucien (1505). The four wings of the palace, as they now stand, facing the four cardinal points, extend over a vast space. The south wing is curious from the quaintness of its arrangement; two square turrets, placed almost at the two extremities, vary its rather commonplace appearance; in the centre, is the entrance gateway, supposed to be the fragment of a heathen temple. The baths, which were enriched with mosaics, marble and gold; the famous gallery; the chamber where Lucien was assassinated; and many other historical apartments, have been destroyed. The great Grimaldi hall is thirty feet in height, twenty paces in length, and twelve in breadth. Frescoes, attributed to Orazio di Ferrara, decorate its walls and ceiling. The colossal chimney-piece is said to have been hewn out of a single block of stone; its fluted columns, helmets and armour, are surmounted by two angels unrolling a fillet, inscribed with the words, "Qui dicit se nosse Deum et mandata ejus non custodit, mendax est." The whole is finished with exquisite workmanship.

This hall of the Grimaldi's, which is now fast falling into decay, was till late years, the scene of a ball, always given by the Princes on the festival of Sta. Devota, the inhabitants, both rich and poor, being invited en masse. The rich danced all evening on one side of the hall, and the peasants on the other, neither ever passing an imaginary boundary, while the Prince and the grandees looked down from a gallery.

Beyond the hall is a desolate suite of rooms, which were pillaged and turned into a barrack at the time of the revolution and have never been restored since. In the last of these rooms, which must once have been rich with gilding and fresco, the custode tells you that a Duke of York, brother of a King of England, died. He was taken ill at sea, when off Monaco, and the Prince offered him a refuge in his palace, where he expired. Afterwards a ship came, and his remains were removed to England with great honours. In recognition of the hospitality their duke had received there, some prisoners belonging to Monaco, who were taken by the English in the French war, were immediately released. The chamber is called "the Duke of York's room" to this day. A number of ill-painted pictures are placed there, which were removed during a fire, from the convent near the Boschetto.

The Courtyard of the palace is very picturesque, its sides having cloisters and friezes covered with ancient frescoes. The west wing is approached by a handsome twisted staircase, at the foot of which is an old well. The east wing contains the apartments, still occupied by the Prince's family during their visits to Monaco; these are not shewn, but are said to be worth seeing, though they can scarcely, as the custode declares, contain "Une galerie toute pleine des tableaux de Raffaele." The north wing contains the domestic chapel.

A passage between the northern and eastern wings leads to the private gardens of the prince, which consist of terraces of aloes and geraniums, bordered with myrtle and thyme, overlooking a lovely view of the bay. Behind are the old bastions and fortifications, among which is the famous "Saraval," which withstood many a siege in the time of the old princes, though now a single cannon, well placed on the Tête du Chien, which frowns above the chateau, might soon do such execution, as would force the town to surrender. The rocks below the garden are covered with a perfect forest of prickly pears, the fruit of which is gathered by a man let down from the wall in a basket. The aloes, which are truly magnificent, generally flower when they attain their fifteenth year, and then die, leaving a numerous progeny behind them. The gardens are shewn in the absence of the family, on presenting a card to the porter of the palace, who for a fee of two or three francs will procure the necessary order from the commandant of the town.

On the east of the town are some baths, pleasantly situated amid groves of Coruba trees, and much resorted to during the hot months.

Amongst the many terrible scenes to which the palace of Monaco has been witness, the most startling was the death of Prince Lucien in 1523, who having gained possession of his sovereignty by the murder of his predecessor and brother, John II, was in turn assassinated by his nephew Bartholomew Doria of Dolceaqua, in his own house, and in the bosom of his hitherto prosperous family. The event is thus described by Gioffredo:

"Among the sisters of Lucien, one, called Françoise, had married Luke Doria, Seigneur of Dolceacqua. During her widowhood Françoise had, on the 19th Dec. 1513, made her will; to this, on the 15th Octr. 1515, she added a codicil, by which she appointed her children to be her heirs, and named Augustin Grimaldi, Bishop of Grasse, and Lucien Grimaldi of Monaco, her brothers, with Ansaldo Grimaldi of Genoa, as her executors. After the death of Françoise, Bartholomew, her eldest son, complained of his uncle Lucien, as having delayed to pay the portion due to him of his mother's inheritance, and soon, blinded by avarice and hatred, he resolved to kill his uncle, and by a base stratagem, to seize the castle of Monaco. Some time before the execution of this criminal enterprise, he sent some of his followers, who were acquainted with his designs, to the Port of Hercules, several of whom were subjects of his cousin the famous Andrea Doria, Seigneur of Oneglia. Bartholomew begged Lucien to allow them to stay at Monaco, since they could not remain safely in his own domains, owing to a quarrel, and in this manner skilfully secured the success of his schemes.

The imprudent Lucien received these secret agents at

F

Monaco, and soon after, his nephew informed him that he intended going to Lyons to meet the King of France, in the hope of obtaining an honorable appointment in his Milanese expedition. Apparently with this object also, Bartholomew arrived at the Port of Hercules, and from thence forwarded a letter to his uncle which Andrea Doria had sent him from Lyons, in which, after having urged him to repair to France, he said, "that it was time to execute the project he knew of." These equivocal words subsequently gave rise to a suspicion that the illustrious admiral had connived at the murder, the more so because his galleys presented themselves before the spot, after the consummation of the crime.

Bartholomew, while pretending to go to Lyons, returned to Dolceacqua to make preparations. At his request, Lucien on Saturday the 22nd August sent one of his brigantines to Ventimiglia to transport his nephew with his suite and goods to the Port of Hercules, where Bartholomew proposed to take leave of him, and thence to continue his journey. On his arrival, Bartholomew was asked by his uncle to hear mass; he declined, saying he had already heard it. Lucien then went thither alone, and his nephew remained during the interval in the gallery of the palace holding a secret interview with his followers. After mass, they went to dinner. The place of honour was given up to Bartholomew, but he found it impossible to eat anything, and it was evident from the preoccupation of his mind, the paleness of his countenance, and the singular expression of his features, that he was meditating some dark and criminal project. Lucien ascribed his nephew's state to a passing sadness, and after vainly pressing him to eat, placed one of his grandchildren in his arms in order to distract his attention; but Doria began to tremble so violently, that the child was obliged to be taken away, as he was unable to hold it.

Such strange conduct might have awakened suspicion in the attendants, but it failed to do so. On leaving the table Bartholomew requested Lucien to furnish him with instructions for his pretended journey to France, and for this purpose they went into a small room at the end of the gallery, where Lucien was in the habit of writing and transacting business. Whilst they were thus engaged, the major domo came to inform his master that he perceived four galleys approaching Monaco. These Bartholomew described as belonging to his cousin Andrea Doria's squadron, and he immediately wrote to the commandant to beg him to enter the port that he might receive an important communication. He shewed the letter to Lucien, and then entrusted it to the major domo, requesting him to carry it to its destination with an armed boat; by this means he contrived to send from twelve to fourteen men away from the palace as necessary for arming the long boat.

August 22, 1523. These measures being taken, Bartholomew sent away all the servants who were in the gallery, except one black slave who would not withdraw. Lucien sat down near the table, while his nephew, remaining standing, began to write, when an assassin from San Remo, who had accompanied Doria, entered the room, followed by one of his accomplices. Nearly at the same moment, the black slave who had refused to go away, from being accustomed never to quit his master, heard him cry out in a frightful manner, repeating the words, "Oh traitor, oh traitor;" when hurrying to the room and half opening the door without daring to enter it, he saw Doria throwing Lucien down on the ground, thrusting a poniard into his neck, and mutilating his body with a thousand blows. The followers of the assassin, who were on the watch, ran towards the room, armed to the teeth, and surrounded Bartholomew, who, leaving the corpse of his victim, sallied forth, sword in hand, crying out, Ammazza! ammazza! slay! slay! This cry was repeated by his men, and by others whom he had sent beforehand to Monaco; halberds and javelins were taken down from the armoury of the guard-room, and the few servants who happened to be at this hour in the palace were driven out. Thus Bartholomew and his associates made themselves masters of the greatest part of the vast building, but they could not gain possession of the great terrace, whither some of the servants had retreated, crying out, To arms! To arms! a cry which was answered at once by the inhabitants, who rushed armed towards the castle. Dolceacqua and his men quickly closed the gates, and made the sign which had been agreed upon, to the galleys anchored off the Capo d'Aglio, a signal which was not however perceived by them.

The inhabitants now forced the gates of the palace and attacked the assassins who had fortified themselves within it. Then Bartholomew shewed himself to the assailants, and besought them to hear him. He began by a protestation that in all he had done, he had only acted in the name of Marie de Vinol, the legitimate sovereign of the country, and, he added, that in three hours, four hundred men would arrive to keep the place in the name of this lady, from whom Monaco might expect, he said, the best treatment and the most signal advantages. At the same time, he caused the corpse of Lucien to be dragged half-way down the staircase, because the inhabitants would not believe in the death of their Seigneur.

Bartholomew's arguments were not listened to: the people in one body charged him with having done them great injury, and tried to seize his person. It was a critical position on both sides; on the one hand Doria's followers found themselves in the most imminent danger, in case the promised and expected succour failed to arrive; on the other the inhabitants were extremely uneasy in knowing that the murderer had fortified himself with the greater part of his men in the most inaccessible part of the castle, while the rest were scattered about the town, and that he expected every moment to be relieved by the galleys of the enemy. In the midst of these fears and anxieties, Bartholomew offered to retire with his men, provided his life were ensured, and the people gave their consent.

The Bishop of Grasse, brother of the victim, at a later time, directed an active pursuit to be made after the criminal, who perished in attacking the castle of Penna, defended by his implacable enemy. As to Andrew Doria, who was with some reason suspected of being implicated in the conspiracy, he could neither escape the severe condemnation of his contemporaries, nor the blame of history. His presence at the Port of Hercules some days previously, his letter to Bartholomew, his galleys arriving at the very hour when the crime was committed, as if to have a share in it, and ensure its impunity or success; are circumstances which clearly prove, that there must have been some secret understanding between the cousins."

CASTELLARE, THE CAPE ST. MARTIN, AND ROCCABRUNA.

Dec. 24.

CASTELLARE is usually one of the first expeditions made from Mentone, as well as one of the most characteristic and picturesque.

Opposite the Hotel des Quatre Nations, a dirty little path diverges from the street, between two walls, overhung on either side with oranges. Following its windings, you emerge at the foot of the yellow tufa rocks behind the town, up which a paved donkey-path winds by many shallow steps, to the high olive terraces, from whence even the cemetery of Mentone appears to be left deep below in the valley, while a wide expanse of blue sea rises above it. The scenery is thoroughly Italian, especially one point where a broad umbrella-pine shades the rock, while behind stands a white cottage in a berceau of vines, backed by the magnificent mountain barrier of St. Agnese.

As the path enters the pine woods, these mountains develope new beauties at every step, and most lovely is the view towards evening, when the blue peaks, with the Saracenic castle on their highest summit, are seen relieved by the red stems of the old pine-trees, and the rich undergrowth of heath and myrtle. The trees are full of linnets, which the natives call " trenta cinques," from the constant sound of their note being " trenta-cinque—trenta-cinque," and as the path is a high way to the mountain olive gardens, the air resounds with the cries of the donkey drivers, "Ulla" ("Allez") go on, and "Isa" (for shame), remonstrances which the donkeys constantly require to induce them to amble along with their heavy burdens of oil-casks, or loads of olives and wood, and, in addition to these, one or two children often clinging on behind. All the peasants turn round to salute those they meet, with a pleasant "bonjour," and a kindly feeling towards strangers, which is very unlike the bad reputation they had during the last century, when the inhabitants of Castellare were quite celebrated for their cruelty, and for the cupidity which led them to murder numbers of emigrants, as they were attempting to escape into Sardinia during the French Revolution, by the unfrequented paths of these desolate mountains.

Castellare is 1350 feet above the sea, and from its elevated position, is a onspicuous object long before you reach it; the houses and tower of the church rising above the feathery olives. The last part of the way is up a steep path, which ends at the entrance of the central and most picturesque of the three little streets of the town; this is very like the old street at Mentone, but is lined by even filthier houses, and redolent of even more disgusting smells. A little coloured campanile is perched upon a house-top near its entrance, and several dingy neglected chapels, belonging to different confraternities, remain with closed doors and grated windows, through which you may descry the decaying pictures, and the collections of tinselled lanthorns and ragged banners, which are left to rust and moth, till the next annual festa of their patron saint, when they are carried out in grand procession. At the entrance of this street on the right, is a quaint kind of piazza, with an old tree, of unusual size for this country, in its centre, from which you gain a view of the ruined entrance of a second street, having tall weather-beaten houses, which stand out against the rugged peaks of the mountains beyond, on one of whose lower slopes is the grey citadel of Castiglione.

Beyond a narrow archway is another miniature piazza, which contained the abode of the once famous family of Lascaris, who ruled this, with almost every other mountain village in the neighbourhood. On one side is the principal church with its tall red tower, and in the little valley below are two old chapels, dedicated to St. Antonio and St. Sebastiano, the latter a very old Romanesque building, with a round apse. Altogether Castellare is full of antiquated beauty, and many a picture might be made of its old buildings, and background of distant mountains and olive gardens, by an artist who does not object to a crowd of dirty people, almost as picturesque as their habitations; for in Castellare no one seems to have any thing to do all day long, and the whole population fluctuated to and fro between us, as five of us sat drawing, four at one end of the town, and one at the other; the former proving in the end the greater attraction, for one child exclaimed, as an excuse for not staying to watch the drawing of the solitary artist, " E molto bella, signora, ma gl'altri vi sono quattro"! One old man in particular hovered round us mysteriously the whole day, and discoursed learnedly on our work; till at last, when he appeared at a window we had sketched, and which the children had long since recognized as "La finestra del maestro," we discovered him to be the unfortunate Italian schoolmaster, who had been ejected since the annexation of Castellare to France, and was now left without occupation, on the world. A member of our party who sat near the door of a Café, heard the inmates discoursing furiously in French, upon this and other miseries consequent upon the change of rulers, which they had only just become aware of; the heavy French taxes not having been enforced till the commencement of the New Year. On observing the foreigner, the landlord gave the grumblers a signal, upon which the conversation was abruptly transferred to patois, probably from a newly-awakened dread of the espionage which is so keenly felt in these lately acquired dominions of the Emperor.

Castellare has many more traces of a Spanish government, than the villages nearer to the high road, and the world. *Uersted.* "Your Excellency," for instance, still takes at Castellare, the place of Signor or Monsieur.

In January and February, the terraces under the olives near Castellare, are gay with purple anemones, narcissus, and many other spring flowers. Among our visitors while drawing here, was the priest, who was quite tipsy, and who roared and shouted like a maniac. In these mountain villages, this is unfortunately no unusual occurrence. The other day a gentleman asked a peasant at Esa if any carriage had ever been up the rocky way to the town. "Only one," was the answer, "and that was the other day, when it went to take the priest prisoner." The priest of Esa was tried in a closed court at Nice, for secret crimes committed in his isolated cure, and was condemned to the galleys for life.

The walk back from Castellare may be varied by turning off at the chapel of St. Sebastiano, and taking the path through the valley on the other side; this path emerges on the hill above the cemetery of Mentone; but it is longer than the other, and more difficult to follow in its windings.

Another of the short excursions from Mentone is that to the Capo Martino, or Cape St. Martin, the wooded promontory, which is so conspicuous in all the views from the Genoa side of the town.

It is about two-miles-and-a-half to the point of the Cape by the shortest way, but the distance may be lengthened, and the road varied, by ascending the hill, and seeing the view on the other side; by wandering through the many woodland paths which cross the peninsula in every direction; or by following the Monaco road. On leaving Mentone by the Nice road, the torrent of Carei or Careye, is crossed by an iron bridge, bordered on each side by a tropical looking mass of aloes and prickly pear, and possessing a fine view of the mountains with the castellated crag of St. Agnese. Then, passing on the right the Hotel de Londres, the road reaches the torrent of Boirigo or Bouriques, where there is only a long wooden bridge for footpassengers, donkeys and carriages being left to splash as best they can. The highway now runs through an avenue of oleanders, on the left of which is the sea, and on the right, first the house of Count Alberti, whose wife is the last representative of the historical and almost royal family of Lascaris, and then the long wall of what is called "Les Jardins du Prince," though his actual garden, long since deeply mortgaged, is further on, while the building in this garden was once a convent, "La Madone," whose foundation dates from the xvth century. The dark chapel of the Virgin attached to the end of the building, and shaded by a palm tree, still keeps up its annual fair and festa and attracts its processions.

Here the English artist, Mr. Alfred Newton, is making a picture, in which the sunshine streaming through the magnificent overhanging pine trees upon golden oranges, and a blue dancing sea, will give to those who see it in the London Exhibition, a pleasant as well as true idea of Mentone.

This spot, though called a garden, is nothing but a wilderness of heath and myrtle, yet is well worth visiting. Entrance may always be obtained, either at the green door in the wall opposite the sea, or at the house near the chapel.

Just beyond is Carnoles, the decaying villa of the Princes of Monaco, with an ill-kept garden, abounding in beautiful flowers, bouquets of which may be bought in the gardener's cottage adjoining. The house built on a much larger scale by Prince Antoine I. was partly destroyed by Honorius V. Opposite, on the sea shore, exposed to the elements, are the remains of an object, which looks like a worn-out waggon, but which was once the carriage of the hated Florestan, from which he was forced to descend by his ex-subjects, when, on his last visit to Mentone, they compelled him to believe that they would not always be slaves.

The next orange gardens on the right, are those of the ancient family of St. Ambroise, of which the Abbè St. Ambroise is considered the most learned, as well as the best priest in Mentone.

Here are some fragments of Roman masonry and a sepulchral chapel, supposed to have been once a Roman temple, dedicated to Diana. A mutilated inscription bears the words—

TERTVLLINO
E   V
— VLLINUS.

Local tradition declares that this is the burial place

of the Roman general Manlius, and of hundreds of others, who fell in a great battle fought on this spot. The name Carnoles is said to have its origin in "Champs de Carnage."

The Ponte del Unione, built in 1860, to commemorate the annexation to France, crosses the torrent which comes down from Gorbio. Here are some of the finest orange gardens in the neighbourhood, and a little beyond this the lane leading to the Cape, branches off to the left from the high road. The direct path mounts a hill, and then loses itself in the many paths which intersect the pine-woods, at a point near which are some remains of a Roman wall, supposed to be relics of the little town of Limone, mentioned in the itinerary of Antoninus, and decided by antiquarians to have been situated on the Cape St. Martin. But a nearer way to the point itself, is the second turn to the left after leaving the high road, which diverges through splendid orange-groves to join a path through the wood, at the foot of the hill; this path was once the high road to Nice, and occupies the site of the old Roman way.

A circular space in the wood marks the site of the "Aristocrat's Tree," whither the gentry of Mentone were accustomed to resort every summer evening before the Revolution, and beneath which it was the fashion to sit round, drinking coffee, "making conversation," and playing at cards. When the revolution came, the aristocrats all escaped across the neighbouring frontier, but the tree which had given them shelter so long, was considered "perdu," and was cut down and chopped to pieces by the republicans, under the brother of the celebrated Robespierre. The pyramid on the left of the path owes its existence to the gratitude of an Englishman, who was cured long ago of a dangerous illness at Mentone, but the inscription which marked it is now effaced, and his name is lost, though some believe it was that Duke of York, who once lived in the Pavilion des Princes, near the Madone.

Several villas are now being built here, and a new colony seems likely to be made by the higher classes of the Mentonese population, who will seek here a cool resort during the hot summer months.

The point is a reef of black and jagged rocks, overgrown with samphire, and washed alternately from either side of the bay by grand waves, which break in perfect mountains of foam upon their sharp edges, with a roar like that of cannon.

The Cape St. Martin is the centre of the Old Principality, and the whole of the tiny kingdom of the Grimaldis may be seen from it, guarded in front by the sea, and behind by the mountains. But the view extends on either side, far beyond the limits of the State; on the left, first Mentone is seen through the tall pines, its houses rising terrace-like to the fine tower of its church; beyond is Ventimiglia with its frontier castle on a projecting rock, while the same mountain chain ends in the houses and church of Bordighera, which look as if they were cut out in white paper, against the deep blue sky. On the right is Turbia, with its Trophæa Augusti, throned high among the mountains, and beyond, a succession of little sandy coves, and coruba-clad promontories: the rock-built town of Monaco, with its fine palace, and hanging gardens, nestling at the foot of the purple rock, known as the Tête de Chien. Behind, above the cape itself, covered with pines and olives, rise the peaks of Mont Garillon and Mount Boudon and the castle of St. Agnese.

It would be difficult to exaggerate the beauty of the Pine wood into which the path now ascends, through an undergrowth of myrtle, rosemary, genista, euphorbia, mediterranean heath, and the different varieties of cistus. Each group of trees serves to frame a new view of mountain peak, or sea and headland. Deep down below on the western side of the cape is a chine, equally remarkable for its views and for the abrupt red rocks which shut it in on one side. In the centre of the promontory buried among the woods are the ruins of the convent of St. Martin, which gave its name to the cape, now consisting only of a few low walls, and the apse of the gothic church, but beautiful from their situation, and the exquisite views of blue mountains which are seen through the golden green of the Pines. At the time when the Saracens were attacking the shores of Liguria, the nuns of this convent, aware of their danger, extracted a promise from the inhabitants of the neighbouring town of Roccabruna, that at the first sound of their convent bell they would fly armed to their assistance. But the abbess distrusting their promise, determined to prove their fidelity, and rang the bell on the very first night, to see if they would come. The people of Roccabruna hurried down immediately, and finding no Saracens, received the blessing of the abbess and retired, feeling angry and insulted. The abbess twice repeated this experiment with success, but on the fourth night when the people of Roccabruna heard the convent bell, they no longer thought it worth while to take any notice, and staid quietly at home. At dawn, the convent was a smoking ruin, and all the nuns were carried off by the Saracens.

Three miles from Mentone, above the road to Nice, amid huge yellow rocks, the debris of a landslip of centuries, stands the town of Roccabruna, the third place in the Old Principality, and one of those for which the Princes of Monaco, through many generations, were forced to do homage on bended knee, first to the Dukes of Savoy, and afterwards to the Kings of Sardinia. This was originally a stronghold of the famous family of Lascaris, who sold it to Charles Grimaldi in 1353 for 16,000 florins, from which time it followed the fortunes of the other Grimaldi possessions till 1848, when the tyranny of its princes, long endured in silence, forced it to seek with Mentone the protection of Sardinia. In 1860 it was annexed to France, and now forms part of the Department des Alps Maritimes.

Tradition tells that Roccabruna was once situated high upon the mountain which now overhangs it, but, that one night the inhabitants went to bed as usual, and in the morning awoke to find the view from their windows quite changed, and the situation of their town entirely different, the whole town, with its houses, gardens, chateau, and church, having quietly slid down to its present site, but so gently, that the position of no single building was disturbed, and no single inhabitant awakened by the move. No one has ventured to assign a date to the event, and the belief probably arose, from the strange manner in which the great tufa rocks, when they fell from their bed in the mountain above, spared the buildings of the town, beyond and among which they lie. From the approach to Roccabruna from Mentone, by the windings of the Nice road, there is a most picturesque view of the straggling town, with its brightly coloured houses, crowned by the chateau, and a solitary palm tree overhanging the olive terraces, and nestling in the purple shadow of Mount Agel. A staircase leads up to the low, narrow, fern-clothed gate of the town, through which you enter the steepest streets imaginable, running up almost perpendicularly to the old castle of the Lascaris; from whose keep there is a fine view over Monaco and Mentone. In one of the ruined chambers is a curious piscina, with an inscription now almost effaced.

The yellow rocks have a curious effect, mingled with the old buildings, which are perched on and around them. The principal church has been newly adorned with a large presépio, where, in a forest of moss and weeds, prettily woven together, a doll virgin in pink glazed calico, is receiving the congratulations of a number of other dolls, the principal figure being a little blue shepherdess, who is making her curtsey in front of the sacred persons, whilst all her little cotton wool sheep, with similar intent, are flocking down behind her through the moss; Herod, meanwhile, in gorgeous attire, surrounded by his guards, sits grimly in the back-ground, and gloomily surveys the pastoral scene.

On the festa of Notre Dame de la Neige, a curious procession takes place, which dates almost from the middle ages, in which the passion of our Saviour is represented; peasants taking the parts of Pontius Pilate, Herod, Sta. Veronica, St. Mary Magdalene, &c. The costumes are very absurd, but the actors go through their parts with imperturbable gravity.

The return to Mentone should be varied by taking the Vieille Route, which branches off near the church, along the olive terraces to the left of the town, and re-enters the high road near the Prince's Gardens. It is a wild, narrow mountain-path winding through old olive woods, carpetted here and there with pale blue periwinkle, and showing lovely glimpses of the bay, with the town of Mentone. A tiny chapel half-way has some quaint old frescoes of the Resurrection, where the Virgin is represented sheltering a number of souls under her cloak, while the rest are resignedly going off to Purgatory.

CHRISTMAS AND THE NEW YEAR.

Jan. 2, 1861.

CHRISTMAS has come and gone, but there has been no outward sign of it here. The splendid nosegay of lemon-blossom and lavender-coloured periwinkles, which we brought home from Roccabruna on Christmas eve, had nothing in it to remind one of the holly and miseltoe at home, nor have the gorgeous salvias, coronellas, and golden flowering mimosas on which we look in the garden beneath our windows. On Christmas morning, Françoise appeared looking very weary and exhausted, and on enquiry, we found that she had been up all night assisting at the birth of the Bambino, in the church of St. Michaele—but, it was a " bambino molto piccolo quest anno," she said, adding, that though the bambino itself was already arrived, the wise men were not expected before the 6th. The ideas of many of the people on religion are most extraordinary. A lady at Maison Viale, was reading to Rosetta her cook, at her own desire, from the Gospels, when she came to the account of the star in the East. "Ah, the star," said Rosetta, " that is what the Jews believe in." "No," said the lady, " on the contrary, that is just what the Jews do *not* believe in." " Ma, Signora, con tutto rispetto," persisted Rosetta, " the Jews *do* believe in it, for my last master had a friend who was a Jew, and who used to fast a great deal, and one night my master's friend said to me, 'Look out, Rosetta, and tell me when the first star begins to shine, because then it will be lawful for me to eat,' therefore, you see, Signora, that it is quite evident the Jews *do* believe in the star." Rosetta listens eagerly to the Bible when it is read, though it is so perfectly new to her, that she roars with uncontrollable laughter at what she considers the ludicrous facts (such as the mistakes of the disciples), and is quite as ready to cry over the affecting ones. When her mistress asked her why she never went to church, she answered unhesitatingly, " parce que vous allez si souvent, que vous faites l'aumône pour moi, Mademoiselle," but, at the same time, she has the greatest admiration of the goodness of others, and says she has had the happiness " de tomber entre trois Dieux," meaning thereby, her mistresses and their old-fashioned English maid-servant.

A Christmas treat was prepared by the English Chaplain for some of the native children, made of cakes, stuck with olives and pieces of garlic, but when the time came to give them away, the cakes were found to have been stripped of these dainties, which some of the children had discovered beforehand, and had eaten surreptitiously, being unable to resist the temptation.

On Thursday 27th, we had a walking party to the Annunziata, which is about two miles from Mentone, and is reached by a path which turns off on the left from the Monti road, a little way out of the town. It is a beautiful wild mountain ascent, with seven Stazione chapels rising in rich mouldering colour, amid the wild chrysanthemums on the tufa rock. Half-way up, some grey fragments of monastic buildings, half buried among the broom and cistus, are the outposts of the Monastery, whose buildings, picturesquely grouped amid tall pines, crown the top of the hill. This is one of the many places here which are supposed to be haunted, and the "revenants" are those of seven monks, its last inhabitants, who, the natives say, were "très, très malheureux," though why they were so excessively unhappy, no one seems quite to know. No peasant will pass the Annunziata at night, and few walk along the Cabruare valley beneath in the dark, without declaring that they see strange fitful gleams of light stream through the convent windows, amid which the seven lean faces of the malheureux monks are seen pressed against the iron grating; and even on the festa of the Annunziata, when the whole convent is freely thrown open to any who choose to enter, few among the numerous pilgrims will ever avail themselves of the permission. We did not take the key, and the cold wind, which rushed out upon us, through the grated windows of the chapel, did not seem inviting for a closer inspection of the place.

The family of the syndic, Monsieur de Monleon, are buried at the Annunziata. Some friends of ours, who had been invited to the ceremony, gave us a curious description of the funeral of his first wife. All the mourners had first assembled at night in the drawing-room of the house, and thence, first, all the relations bearing torches, and then all the visitors and common people, with lighted candles, followed the coffin to the church, where the funeral service was performed. After this the mourners accompanied the coffin half-way down the street, and then they abandoned it to the care of seven "white brethren," who bore it to the little chapel of St. Benoit, where they watched it till morning, after which they carried it, no one following, and without any further service, for burial at the Annunziata. Our friends said that it was sad to see the change in the white brethren; how they had at once thrown off their mourning faces, and were laughing and joking as they came back; and how, when once the service in the church was over, no one seemed to care any more about the poor body, or what became of it.

All the way-side chapels are burial places of old families, but of these there are very few representatives now remaining at Mentone; most of the existing aristocracy date only from the French revolution. Of two families which once possessed almost sovereign power in the neighbourhood, descendants are still extant, but those of the family of Vento, of whom Emmanuel Vento sold the sovereignty of Mentone to Charles Grimaldi, in the year 1346, are now reduced to such poverty, that the son is obliged to give music lessons; and the daughters to go out as governesses; while of the family of Lascaris, who built almost all the castles in the neighbourhood, and of whom Guiglielmo Lascaris, Count of Ventimiglia, sold Roccabruna to the same Grimaldi, for 16,000 golden florins, only one, a female descendant, still exists, who is married to Count Alberti. She has two houses in the town, and a villa near the Prince's gardens, and she still retains the old castle of Gorbio, whither she and her husband sometimes retire in the summer.

The Mentonese are remarkable for the frequency with which they change their names. This has often been the consequence of the change of government in the principality. The Gastaldy family boast that their name has existed in almost every language: first they were Spaniards, Gastaldo; then they were French, Gastalde; then they were Italian, Gastaldi; and now they are,—has the name an English enunciation?—Gastaldy.

Charades are quite the fashion here this winter, and no

party seems to be thought complete without them, till for those who are expected to take a part in them, acting has become one of the necessary fatigues of the day. "Scarlet" and "Digest" were two words which went off with great success the other day, also "Furbellows," which was a parody on the climate of Mentone. The first scene represented a happy family of mother, son, and two daughters, sitting out in their garden under the olive-trees, perfectly exhausted by the heat. In aggravation of their sufferings, the son read aloud a letter, which had been just received from an English cousin, describing the intense cold in their own country, with the frost, the skating, &c. While they were still in the garden, a telegram was brought in, announcing that the writer of the letter was on his way to join them, in the hope of recovering in a more genial climate from the effects of the cold, and that he would probably arrive that very afternoon. In due time the cousin appeared, wrapped up with the greatest care, and guarded by furs against the imaginary fury of the elements. At first he was enchanted with the warmer temperature, but soon the sudden transition, and his unsuitable attire, caused him to fall down in a fainting fit in the midst of his ecstacies, and the scene closed as the whole family were rushing upon him with scent bottles and fans, the Mentonese donna fanning him over the heads of all the rest. The second scene opened with the next morning, when the habitués of Mentone, aware of the capricious climate, came down warmly clad and well muffled up, but the unfortunate stranger, judging only by the day before, came down in summer coat and white trowsers, and was discovered vainly endeavouring to produce a blaze from the damp wood of the ill-laid fire. Shiverings and murmurings were the order of the day, and the scene fell on the whole party making an onslaught on the fire, with every pair of bellows that can be found in the house. The whole word Furbellows, was a scene of preparation for the Mentone ball.

We have lately had several rather cold nights, with a sharp air and a hot sun by day. Françoise has dilated on some ice she has seen in the streets on her way hither in the early morning, but by the time we are up, it has all disappeared, and the flowers and the sunshine are looking as summery as ever. The high mountains, however, at the back of the town, are covered with snow, and look quite Alpine, and yesterday, when walking upward from the Cabruare valley, the views in the excelsior were quite magnificent, with the change from the rich luxuriant orange-groves beneath, in the gradual ascent of the tufa rocks, to ice and a splendid amphitheatre of snow peaks, beneath which Gorbio lies sheltered on a purple ledge of rock.

On the Jour de l'An, our old postman brought us a present of an almanack, and the milk-woman, Angelina Pastorella, who kissed and hugged Françoise when they met, in compliment to the day, brought with her a letter, directed, "Alla Signora Hare, dalla sua humile Pastorella," and written as follows:—" Signora e Signore. Crederci di mancare al mio dovere, se in questo nuovo anno non vi augurasco una perpetta salute, e tutta sorta di benedizioni celeste e terreste. Agiungendo soltanto che io faccio al cielo miei voti piu cari at piu ardenti par la conservazione dei suoi giorni e della sua salute, spero che il Signore exdisca i miei voti, Angiolina Pastorella."

The servant of one of our neighbours brought her a present, which was highly characteristic of the place. There is no grass here, not a blade, for though the hills are green, they are only made so by the abundance of the thyme, myrtle, and flowers that covers them, so the maid having heard that English people were in the habit of constantly seeing grass in their own country, went up to one of the mountain villages, whence she brought down, with much labour and perseverance, two pots of grass, and presented them to her mistress as a great rarity.

CAVALIERE TRENCA.

In walking down the Rue St. Michael, the passenger's eye is arrested by a large house, on which, over the doorway, is a marble tablet inscribed—

> A CARLO TRENCA
> CAVALIERE COMMENDATORE DEI SANTI MAURIZIO E
> LAZZARO, PRESIDE AL GOVERNO, AGLI STUDI, ALLA
> MILIZIA NAZIONALE DI MENTONE E ROCCABRUNA,
> PER DOTTRINA, PER PATRIA CARITA, PER VIRTU
> PRECLARO; BENEMERITO CARISSIMO
> I MEMORI CONCITTADINI
> 4 GUIGNO 1854.

Then he will ask, who was this Cavaliere Trenca so beloved by his fellow countrymen; and in answer to his questions concerning his life, will come such an outpouring of praise, mingled with recollections of his life, that it may be well to give a short sketch of what that life was.

The Trenca family can trace back its pedigree to the foundation of its native town of Mentone, where one of the first houses which existed was built by one of its members. The great grandfather of Col. Trenca obtained the rank of baron from the king of Poland, but the grandson of the 1st baron was induced to destroy his patent of nobility in 1793, at the time when the terrors of the revolution, often caused the name of aristocrat to be fatal both to the life and fortunes of its possessor. On the maternal side also Cavaliere Trenca was of honorable birth, his mother Felicité Levamis having been taken under the protection of the princesses of Piedmont, when her father Antoine fled from Mentone, to escape the vengeance of the Prince of Monaco, which he had incurred through his devotion to the royal house of Savoy. One of the princesses was godmother to Felicité, who was well educated by her care, and endowed with a marriage portion, which descended to her son Charles.

Nature had bestowed brilliant talents upon Charles Trenca, and these were carefully cultivated by his parents; at Nice, at Marseilles, and at Turin, his education was successfully carried on in turn, and at the age of eighteen he had not only been well grounded in all the more solid branches of learning, but had become distinguished among the musicians of his native land by his musical compositions, which were chiefly on sacred subjects. At eighteen he was appointed Lieutenant of the Guard by Honorius V. of Monaco, and in the following year was married to Mademoiselle Francoise de Monleon, the daughter of an old and noble Mentonese family. In 1828 he was appointed Captain of the Carabineers, and in 1831 Portuguese Consul in the Principality. But in the same year his discontent with the government of the Princes of Monaco was first openly manifested, and it soon became the great object of his life to free the people of his native place from the heavy burdens which were inflicted on them by the tyranny of their rulers. The feelings of Charles Trenca, were too clearly manifested to escape the notice of the ruling powers, and led in 1835 to his being deprived of his military rank; but this was voluntarily restored to him by Prince Honorius V. two years later; and his successor Florestan, anxious to gain Trenca as a partisan, chose him as one of the deputation which was sent to Turin to receive the investiture of Mentone, Roccabruna and their dependencies, while the Duke of Valentinois, the hereditary prince, chose him as his equerry during his stay at Turin, in preference to all his other officers. Here Charles Trenca received the cross of a knight of the order of St. Maurice and St. Lazarus, and was admitted to a private audience with Charles Albert, in which, after the king had questioned him on the political state of Mentone, he took leave of him with these words: " M. Trenca je suis charmé de vous avoir connu, si je puis être utile à vous ou à votre famille j'en saisirai toujours l'occasion avec plaisir."

The honours conferred upon him in Sardinia, induced the prince of Monaco to offer M. Trenca the appointment of Comptroller General of the Finances on his return home, an office which he accepted with reluctance. The year following he again accompanied the Duke of Valentinois to Turin, and on this occasion was entrusted by the Sardinian Minister of Foreign Affairs with the delicate mission of sounding his master as to his intentions regarding the cession of Monaco to Sardinia. The suspicion which this difficult task threw upon his fidelity, led to an accusation that he was in secret correspondence with the Sardinian government. Trenca, who had never concealed his sympathy with Sardinia, and his desire to establish more intimate relations between that court and his own, immediately resigned his offices, and called for a public enquiry into his conduct; but both were equally refused by the Prince of Monaco, who, to show his continued confidence in him, conferred on him the additional office of High Treasurer. In this and in all his other employments, his one object still continued to be the interests of the people, and to raise his voice against the daily increasing burdens which the tyranny of the government imposed upon them. At length 1847 arrived, when the people had to choose between absolute ruin and a revolution; and then, when once more Charles Trenca exhorted the Prince of Monaco to save himself, and secure the gratitude of his subjects, by a generous change of conduct, the Prince only replied by abruptly depriving him of all his offices, and dismissing him at once from his favour. Thus, without seeking it, he was released from all his oaths of allegiance, and when a bloodless revolution had given freedom to his native land, Trenca at once found himself looked upon as the chief mover in the provisional government, where he continued to maintain a patriotic course of conduct, from which his former masters, now only too sensible of what they had lost, vainly endeavoured to withdraw him. The gratitude of his fellow citizens first appointed him Colonel Commander-in-Chief of the municipal guard, and President of the government, and afterwards sent him as the head of the Commissioners appointed to carry to Turin and Paris the unanimous vote of the people for annexation to Sardinia. This deputation met with a favorable reception at Turin, and left it, animated by hopes of a speedy and successful result at Paris; but there they found that their adversaries had raised every possible obstacle against them. After a month, however, of incessant toil, they were overcome by M. Trenca's unwearied efforts, and he had the joy of announcing to his eagerly-expectant fellow citizens, that their wishes were accomplished. On this the brightest day of his life, he exclaimed, "Quel triomphe, je suis heureux j'ai sauvé mon pays, jè puis mourir maintenant et entonner le cantique du prophète, nunc dimitte," &c. After winding up the affairs of the annexation, the Commissioners returned to Mentone, where they were greeted with the utmost enthusiasm by the whole population, who rushed out in crowds along the Genoa road to meet them. A triumphal arch, with the inscription " Ai deputati di Mentone e Roccabruna reduci da Torino, la Patria Riconoscente," was erected at the entrance of the town, and the whole population, and the National Guard with music and flags flying, came to the house of M. de Monleon where M. Trenca had alighted, to compliment him on the success of his important mission.

In the following month the provisional government resigned its office into the hands of the commissioner extraordinary of the King of Sardinia, who immediately applied to have the honour of Col. of S.S. Maurice and Lazare conferred upon Trenca, as the most meritorious citizen of Mentone. Soon after this he was appointed by Charles Albert to attend the Marchese Ricci at the Congress of Brussels, of which the object was the amicable settlement of the differences between Austria and Sardinia. At Turin he was again received by his sovereign with the most flattering marks of attention. But the conferences at Brussels were soon cut short by the fatal battle of Novara and the abdication of the king, when Trenca, who was overcome with grief at the misfortunes of his benefactor, flew to Paris to endeavour to arrest the dangers which threatened Mentone in consequence, and obtained from the French court a ratification of their former promises; thence he proceeded to Turin, and after numberless difficulties, he obtained from Victor Emmanuel the decree which united the communes of Mentone and Roccabruna to the division of Nice. The proclamation of this decree, and of the measures for the future government of the country, gave the greatest satisfaction to the people, and the vote of the

Piedmontese Chambers being all that was now wanted to complete legally the desired annexation to Sardinia, Col. Trenca was again chosen to go to Turin on the meeting of Parliament, to bring the subject before it as speedily as possible. Circumstances rendered this a very difficult task, but after some months of vexatious delay, the annexation was almost unanimously agreed to by the Chamber of Deputies; and it had only to be confirmed by the Senate, when the dissolution of the Parliament in November once more caused a delay.

The following year, 1850, M. Trenca again hastened to Turin, and after ten months of the most harassing delays, he was at last able to return to Mentone, with the assurance of the Sardinian ministry, that the vote for the annexation should be fully and legally ratified. Great was the joy of the people when M. Trenca brought them these happy tidings; the day of his return was kept as one of public rejoicing, and a grand banquet was prepared in his honour by his fellow-citizens. The next six months passed quietly away, till another vexatious obstacle to the prosperity of the town arose, from the French government objecting to receive Mentonese vessels bearing the Sardinian flag. This again called M. Trenca to Turin, and from thence to Paris, where, aided by his friend Comte Maurice de Partouneaux, a warm and constant defender of the Mentonese people, he was at last able to overcome all the difficulties raised by designing partisans of the Prince of Monaco, and gained the desired permission, that for the future Mentonese vessels might enter all French ports on the same conditions and under the same flag as the Sardinian ships.

Matters being thus satisfactorily arranged in Mentone, Charles Trenca devoted some months to a political tour in Germany and Russia, after which he gave himself up with new experience to the organization of schools in his native town, and to the improvement of the public instruction in all its branches. His duties as Colonel of the National Guard also occupied a large portion of his time.

The last political transaction in which Trenca took a part, was heading the deputation sent to meet the President of the French republic, Prince Louis Napoleon, at Toulon, where his gracious reception and promises of protection raised the brightest hopes in the minds of all those who were admitted to converse with him. Soon after this Col. Trenca's health began to fail; still he could not be persuaded to leave his work unfinished. " Que je puisse régénérer mon pays," he often said, " et je mourirai content. Je ne demande rien pour moi, mon seul desir est de voir ma patrie affranchie et heureuse." But too soon an attack of typhus fever, supervening upon other maladies, proved fatal; and thus at the age of 52, this good man was lost to his country. His funeral was attended by almost the whole population of Mentone and Roccabruna, headed by the clergy, the national guard, the garrison and the various schools. His praises were rehearsed in sermons preached by the clergy in the churches which were hung with mourning, and in the funeral orations which were pronounced over his grave both in French and Italian. But more lasting than these, or even than the inscription on the tablet, which the whole population of the two communes once more assembled to place (June 4, 1854) over the door of his house, is the feeling of love and respect which still encircles his memory, and which will prevent his name from ever being forgotten in his native town.

THE EASTERN ENVIRONS OF MENTONE.

When the Revolution came, France took possession of Mentone, and the brother of the terrible Robespierre was sent thither " to represent the people, and to guillotine the aristocrats." But fortunately the frontier was not far off, and all the doomed persons fled across it before M. Robespierre could arrive, so that when he came and took up his quarters in the Maison d'Adhemar, he found very little to do. Meanwhile the little colony of royalists established themselves at La Cuze, near the Pont St. Louis, just beyond the frontier, where they lived very comfortably, safe within the republic of Genoa, but still in sight of their own homes. People yet living at Mentone, hand down from the recital of their parents, curious details of the lives of these exiles, who were obliged to live in the most limited space in the maisonettes of the orange gardens, though in the evening all the society met together to play at cards in the principal villa. Among the royalists, was one old man, who had no family, but only a faithful dog, with which he lived quite alone in a little cottage, which still stands above an archway, near the wall overhanging the path by the sea shore to the Rochers Rouges. One night he had been playing at cards as usual, and returned home late with his faithful companion. But soon after the dog returned to the villa, and going to each of the company in turn, by its signs of distress endeavoured to attract their attention. They all decided that something must have happened to its master Monsieur le Bour, as the solitary old man was called, and on going to his cottage to look after him, they found that he had fallen down on the floor in an apoplectic fit, of which he soon afterwards died. The dog refused to leave his body, and even after he was buried, remained by the grave of its master, from which nothing could entice it away; and there, refusing all food, it eventually expired. Afterwards as the French territory extended further along the Riviera, the emigrants were forced to fly to Ventimiglia and finally to Taggia.

At this time the only road through Mentone was that which passed through the Rue Longue, and along the terrace above which the English chaplain's house and Maison Trenca, &c. are now situated. This road continued the whole way from Nice to Genoa, passing sometimes along the sea shore, sometimes high up in the mountains, in both of which situations, traces of it are still to be met with. Madame de Genlis says of it, " En sortant de Nice cette route est parfaitement bien nommée la Corniche ; c'est en effet presque toujours une vraie Corniche, en beaucoup d'endroits si etroite qu'une personne y peut à peine passer. .... Depuis Monaco jusqu' à Menton l'on respire ; le chemin est tres beau. Cette derniere ville est agréable ; elle est entree sur le bord de mer, et l'on y trouve quantités des citronniers et d'oranges, dont l'air est embaumé."

Under the empire this was all changed. A military road from Nice to Genoa was ordered by Napoleon shortly after his coronation in France, but it was only constructed as far as Ventimiglia before his fall cut short its completion. The road along the quay of Mentone was made at this time ; but the most striking memorial of the empire in these parts is the Pont St. Louis, one-mile-and-a-half from Mentone, on the road to Genoa, crossing a frightful abyss between two gigantic rocks, with a single arch of 22 metres span, at the height of 80 metres. The situation of this bridge is striking and romantic in the highest degree, surrounded by tremendous precipices, while in the depth beneath, an old aqueduct, winding along the surface of the rock, carries water from a cascade to the orange gardens near it. The best view of this bridge is from below, where on the terraces of the Villa Naylor, the heliotrope, hanging in masses from the high walls, is in full flower even in December, and where the brilliant salvias, plumbagos and roses with which the garden is filled, form a striking contrast to the wild scenery beyond it.

This place, beautiful as it is, abounds in histories which are each more dreadful than the other.

After the revolution of 1789, bands of peasants and deserters formed themselves into companies in the wild districts of North Italy, and were known as "Barbets." These people, goaded on by misery, were accustomed to rob and murder travellers, and then to hide themselves in the mountains, amongst the ravines and rocks, where none could find them. It is said that one of these Barbets, a peasant by origin, but a deserter from a regiment, took refuge behind the Pont St. Louis, in a cavern, reached only by a tiny path in the rock, and that from thence he attacked and plundered those who passed by. There, he was one evening awaiting a visit from his betrothed, a young girl of Fregonia or Ciotti, his native village, who, ignorant that her lover was an assassin, frequently escaped unobserved from home in order to see him in his hiding place, and console him by her loving words. Whilst he was lying hidden behind a rock, the Barbet heard a footstep coming along the little path, and saw a man approach carrying a small portmanteau. The temptation was too great, and throwing himself upon the unfortunate traveller, he murdered him in an instant. But another scream echoed the death cry of his victim; it was that of the young girl, who arrived at the moment of the fatal act, and having thus witnessed the guilt of her lover, threw herself in despair from the top of the little path and fell into the gulf below the Pont St. Louis. Her body was never found; the Barbet was afterwards taken, but his fate is unknown.

The villa was also the scene of a sad calamity only three years ago, when a young English girl, who had gone out with her sister to see the sunset, fell from the rocks and was killed on the spot. The distress of her family was aggravated by the difficulties which the Mentone officials threw in the way of the removal of the body to the house before the inquest, which was to take place on the following day, and which were only overcome by the personal interest with the syndic of a family who had long been resident in the town. Another tragedy occurred in the same garden, when an English child in a fit of passion, shot the gardener's little son dead upon the spot.

A rugged path under the cliff below the road leads round the Rochers Rouges to a platform whence there is a splendid view of the town, and of the mountains, embracing the distant coast of France, the Estrelles and Antibes, with Monaco, Mont Agel, Turbia, Monts Garillon and Baudon, St. Agnese and the Berceau. The rocks themselves are exceedingly fine both in form and colour; they are overgrown with wild rue, rosemary, euphorbia and delicate painted mallows. In their caverns a great number of the bones of the stag, goat, horse, wild boar, wolf, wild cat and rabbit have been discovered, with an immense quantity of shells of the still existing kinds of fishes. These, and the number of fragments of rude weapons in flint also discovered here, lead to the supposition that these caverns must once have been inhabited by the Troglodytes, described by Strabo and Pliny. This theory is expatiated upon in a pamphlet called "Les Instruments Silex et les Ossements trouvés dans les Cavernes de Menton," by M. Forel, 1860.

On a stormy day, the waves dash up grandly beneath the cliffs in foaming showers of spray, and the water rushing under the rocks, and being forced upwards by the air through their little fissures, produces the most graceful natural fountains.

Beyond the red rocks is a platform containing a little walled-in Gethsemane of olive trees, which quite cover the ground with their black berries. Hence a path winds up the hill to join the Riviera road. The old Genoa road, a mere mule track, still exists in parts nearer the shore, but in some places it has been entirely carried away by torrents and landslips. Theresine says, that when this was the highway to Genoa, accidents never ceased to occur here, and she herself recollects the time when a month never passed without a man or a mule being precipitated into the chasm beyond the Rochers Rouges, and being dashed to pieces. One of the persons who fell into this frightful abyss, escaped and is alive still, and employed on the new road above. One day, Mr. Newton, the artist, was going by this path to his work, with the porter of his hotel carrying a large picture before him. Suddenly, with a loud scream, both man and picture disappeared into one of the chasms. "Were you not terrified for the fate of your picture?" he was asked. "No," he said, "I was so certain that the man must be dashed to pieces, that it never occurred to me to think of the picture at all." However, the man was not at all hurt, and came up grinning, while the picture had a large hole knocked through the middle of it.

Continuing this path with difficulty, on turning the corner of the promontory, one reaches a quaint dilapidated building, with a solitary palm tree and some old cypresses beside it, which still retains traces of rich ancient colour around its windows and doorways, and which has an open loggia covered with frescoes. This is the Palazzo Orenga, which formerly belonged to the noble Genoese family of that name, by whom it was built, and who are now extinct. Its present possessor, Signor Granducci, a wild-looking figure, with shaggy uncombed locks, a red cap with a hood over it, and a long blue cloak which covered him all over, received us with great kindness when we went there, showing us all over the house and into the loggia, whose arches frame an exquisite view of Bordighera. The fine old rooms were in the last stage of decay, the frescoed ceilings having in many places fallen in, and having been replaced by a rough roof of timber, which was insufficient to keep out the wet. The poor old Signor accompanied us when we went away, down the rocky slope, which was quite perfumed by the wild lavender, now (January) in full bloom. He asked us many questions about politics, for his isolation was evidently never broken by a newspaper. Especially was he anxious to know whether there was likely to be a war in Italy this year, because he said, "Si les Autrichiens arrivent, ils nous enverront en Paradis." "Well," was the answer, "if they only do *that*, it will not be much harm." "Mais Monsieur, je ne suis pas trop pressé," muttered the old Signor.

Above the palazzo is the village of St. Mauro, which in French ought to be rendered St. Maur, not St. Maurice, as it has been called since the annexation.

Beyond the brown ruined tower, which stands on the point above the Rochers Rouges, a line of white houses is seen, among the olive-trees above the road. It is worth while to climb up to them, for they form the village of Grimaldi, whose broad sunny terrace is as thoroughly Italian a scene as any in the Riviera, for it is crossed by a dark archway, and lined on one side with bright houses, upon whose walls yellow gourds hang in the sun, with a little church, painted pink and yellow, while on the other is overshadowed by old olive-trees, beneath which is seen the broad expanse of sea, here deep blue, there gleaming silver white in the hot sunshine. Children in bright handkerchiefs and aprons, are always playing about in Grimaldi, and the constant burden of their song, "Tanta di gioia, tanto di contento," while we were drawing there, gave a pleasant idea of their condition.

Beyond Grimaldi the path becomes steeper, and being much exposed, is like a forcing-bed under the hot rays of the sun in the middle of the day. But we were quite repaid for the fatigues of our walk when we reached the top, as the scenery there is almost Alpine, in its bold rocky foregrounds, beneath which yawns the deep black chasm of St. Louis, with a huge cliff frowning above. The cries of the birds, too, and the shouts of the goat-herds were quite like those of Switzerland. Half-way up the gorge an aqueduct winds along the face of the rock, which is often used as a foot-path, though it is none of the safest. The other day, as a lady was walking along here to see the view, she suddenly became giddy from the unguarded height on which she was resting; she caught at the nearest stone to support herself, when, to her horror, it gave way, and, in an instant, she was deluged by a perfect torrent of water, which rushed out above, behind, and around her; for the stone she had seized for safety, had been the plug of the aqueduct. Happily, the gentleman who was with her, had presence of mind to throw himself on his face, and to hold her feet, to prevent her being carried away, and thus they supported themselves till the first fury of the water had subsided. A winding path now skirts the hill to Ciotti Inferiore, where a broken stone arch frames a picturesque view of the Berceau. Above, on the scorched rock, is Ciotti Superiore, a quaint cluster of houses, while the church, quite separated from its village, stands further off on the highest ridge of the mountain. From behind the rock, at the back of the church, the sea-view is truly magnificent, embracing the coast, with its numerous bays, as far as the Estrelles, which turn golden and pink in the sunset; the grand mountain barriers, with all the orange-clad valleys running up into them; and St. Agnese rising out of the blue mist, on its perpendicular cliff. Close at hand a huge projecting rock breaks the whole view, and lights it up with its varied fringe of golden green fir-trees. Ciotti is certainly one of the most striking places near Mentone, and has a wild mountain character of its own that is quite peculiar, yet, even in this high situation, the most lovely narcissus and pink carnations were blooming in January, and a little " Carita " begging girl, was enchanted to sell us a large bunch of them for one soldo, while we were drawing.

GORBIO AND ST. AGNESE.

January 17.

GORBIO is a delightful expedition. The valley of that name is lovely, and presents a whole series of pictures, in its little chapels, with old chestnut-trees overhanging them, in its ruined oil mills and broken bridges. Later in the season it is quite carpeted with brilliant scarlet anemones.

The way thither turns off from the Nice road, by the Madone Convent, close to the Prince's gardens. The village of Gorbio, which is about four miles from Mentone, is wonderfully picturesque in its situation, but is rather disappointing in itself, containing only the usual number of low dark archways, a gloomy church, and the ruined castle of the Lascaris, which retains a Romanesque window in its tower. The figure-artist might find good subjects among the women, who wash round the fountain beyond the village, or the men, performing, as we saw them, a quaint dance, which was chiefly hand-acting, near a terra cotta shrine, beneath an old tree, which here, as at Castellare, forms the outpost of the place. The best view for a sketch is from some boulder stones behind the village, whence it is seen standing on its conical hill backed by the sea, and the promontory of Bordighera.

The annual festa at Gorbio is like that of the other villages, except that here it is the custom for the peasants to present cockades to all the visitors, who are expected to offer some trifling gratuity in return. Lately these cockades have been made of the French colours, and, Italians refusing to wear them, the festas have become the scene of mild popular demonstrations.

The walk from Gorbio to Roccabruna is neither difficult nor fatiguing, and has beautiful views over the pine-clad mountains of St. Agnese on its jagged peak. As we came down upon Roccabruna in the sunset, the dark castle stood out against a sea of gold and a flame-coloured sky, closing the ravine by which we descended. Our walk had been a long one, and it was pleasant to find a refection of wine, and the sugared cakes which are peculiar to Roccabruna, awaiting our arrival, beneath the old crumbling gateway.

January 22.

Up, high up, through woods of pine, with a rich undergrowth of myrtle and tall white heath, winds the donkey-path to St. Agnese. Indeed, there are three paths, all equally beautiful, and with the same wooded character, only the distance is different. That which is generally taken, crosses the torrent Boirigo, near the entrance of the Cabruare valley, whence it begins an abrupt ascent, and fringed with cistus and myrtle, runs along one of the high ridges of the hills, directly towards the great mountain-barriers. The upper parts of these are grey, jagged and broken precipices of perpendicular rock, while their lower slopes are clothed pines, among which rises on the left the village of Gorbio, picturesquely placed in the hollow of a mountain amphitheatre. At length, the path steepens into a staircase, which climbs the rock by the edge of a clear rivulet, beyond which the village of St. Agnese comes suddenly in sight, behind gigantic grey precipices, crowned by the ruins of the Saracenic Castle. The village itself is one long street of low brown ruinous houses, with a solitary campanile rising from them, whose spire, covered with bright red and yellow tiles, is the only patch of colour in the whole landscape. Everything else looks dreary in the extreme, even the pines and myrtle have long since ceased, and scarcely a vestige of verdure enlivens the dead brown of the hills, while, behind, rises a second range of mountains, still more dreary, lurid and barren. To those who ascend hither from the sunny orange-groves of Mentone, it seems incredible that the temperature of St. Agnese is exactly the same as that of Clarens and Montreux, the Italy of Switzerland, yet so it is; though even the church, in its dedication to "Notre Dame de la Neige," bears witness to the character of St. Agnese, as compared with the surrounding villages.

We have been up twice to spend the day. The first time we were lionized over the village by the Curé, who, with the kindness which is invariably shewn by the priests in these mountain solitudes, was anxious to do the honours of his native place. The gaily-painted church, which has a vestibule of the 13th century, contains nothing remarkable. In the adjoining piazza, the little chapel and campanile of St. Carlo is picturesque, with a ruined doorway beside it, which forms the frame-work to a picture of snow-covered mountains, and bright rocks in the foreground, with goats grouped upon them. Those who do not wish for the additional ascent to the castle, may enjoy much the same view from a sunny terrazone, which commands a splendid panorama of the lower mountain ranges, intersected by orange-clad valleys, each with its separate torrent rushing to join the sea, whose vast blue expanse extends in either direction. Here women are always sitting out at work in the sunshine, and it is surprising to see mothers of large families allowing their children to play so close to the edge of the precipice, which is entirely unguarded. Hence, two very steep and stony paths lead down into the Cabruare valley, one descending abruptly to the village itself, the other running along a mountain ridge, by a lonely chapel, bearing inscription to the "Divæ Lucæ," where there is a pretty peasant's fête on the day of Sta. Lucia.

On the highest spur of the mountain, above the village, stand the ruins of the Saracenic castle, now reduced to mere fragments of wall, which almost seem one with the bare grey rock from which they spring. Tradition tells, that a Saracenic chieftain named Haroun, fortified this castle, whence he could observe all that passed on the Roman road below, and pillage what he pleased, occasionally carrying off both the inhabitants and their property, while some of his companions carried on the same system of plunder by sea.

Among the captives thus brought hither, was a Christian virgin named Agnes, whose father and brothers were murdered before her eyes, and who had been seized with her companions on board a vessel which was conveying her to Spain. Her charms induced Haroun to force her to become his bride, and, by her amiable qualities, he was at length convinced of the truth of her religion, which he embraced, and built under the shelter of his fortress, a chapel to her patron saint, which became a place of great resort for the devout. To escape the vengeance of his former companions, Haroun was eventually obliged to escape with Agnes to Marseilles, where his baptism was celebrated with great rejoicings, and where he soon afterwards died. After his flight the Saracens abandoned St. Agnese for ever.

Our second visit was during the festa, when a concourse both of rich and poor, thronged the ascent. We arrived at eleven o'clock, but, by staying to draw at the first point where the village comes in sight, were not in time for the procession, and only heard the distant chantings borne on the wind, and saw the long line of white figures moving slowly along the terrazone above us. Most of the other English were in time to see them emerge from the principal church, and proceed to the little chapel of St. Agnese, where, according to ancient custom, a golden apple is offered to the clergy by the lord of the manor, (Signor Bottini). He always appears heading the procession in court dress, which, till the revolution, was that of Louis xv.; till then, also the golden apple was always stuffed with gold pieces, which were presented to the charities of the place, but now it is a mere matter of form. The greater part of the procession consisted of women, with white handkerchiefs or veils upon their heads, and lighted candles in their hands, headed by the banner of St. Agnes, on which the virgin saint is represented with her lamb. Kneeling along the whole length of the terrace, they chaunted the hymn of St. Agnes in the open air, a sight which is effective at a distance, but which should not be seen too near, or dirt and ugliness may destroy the poetry of the picture. When the procession had returned to the church, some of the women assisted at a very congregational service there, while others proceeded to dance upon the terrace. Several handsome young peasants went about with baskets of flowers, presenting bouquets to the lady visitors, and, those who accepted them, were rather astonished to find that their having done so was equivalent to having accepted the donor as a partner, and that they also were expected to dance. Space was cleared, music struck up, and English and natives were soon mingled together in the mazes of a lively country dance. The bright rapidly moving figures, the rich colouring of the yellow rocks and the old houses, with their purple background of mountains, made a beautiful scene. There was, however, a melancholy absence of costume, little existing, except the ordinary coloured handkerchiefs of the women, and the tall red cap (berretto) of the men. The proceedings were wound up by an accident, which is usually the case on these occasions. A woman, whom they declared to have drunk too much champagne, though it is difficult to imagine where she can have found it in this mountain fastness, fell over the rocks, and was taken up insensible. This morning we have heard that she is dead. It is remarkable, that her only son was killed in exactly the same way and at the same time, three years ago.

We determined to return by Sta. Lucia, in spite of the positive declarations of Theresina Ravellina, who was with us, that we should not do anything of the kind, as she persisted the way was impracticable for her donkeys, all of which we knew was because of a friend, whom she wished to accompany to Cabruare. We insisted on going our own way; but when we had reached the foot of the first range of rocks, Theresina came after us, screaming that we had lost our way, and were not going to Sta. Lucia at all, and as she brought with her two fellow-countrymen to support her assertion, we were obliged to believe her, and toil back after her into the route. Too late we discovered that we *had* been in the right way after all, when she cooly confessed, that as she could not gain her way by fair means, she had taken it by foul.

During the winter wolves frequently appear at St. Agnese, and are a constant subject of terror in this and other of the high mountain villages. Three years ago, a woman was at work in an olive garden near her cottage, in the village of Bera, when a man passed by, who told her that he had seen a wolf going towards her house, in which she had left her baby asleep. She flew home, and, on opening the door, saw a young girl struggling with the wolf upon the floor. *She* too had seen the wolf go towards the cottage, and utterly regardless of herself, had pursued it, in order to save the child. When she arrived, the wolf was on the point of rushing upon the cradle; it regarded her for an instant, and then they closed in a deadly struggle. The girl was very strong, and having contrived to clutch the wolf by the throat, she held it thus, till the mother returned with assistance, when the wolf was killed with a hatchet. Afterwards the mother put the child on her mule, and slinging the dead wolf across the saddle in front of it, took them down to Nice, where making a little exhibition, she collected several hundred francs for the child who had saved her baby.

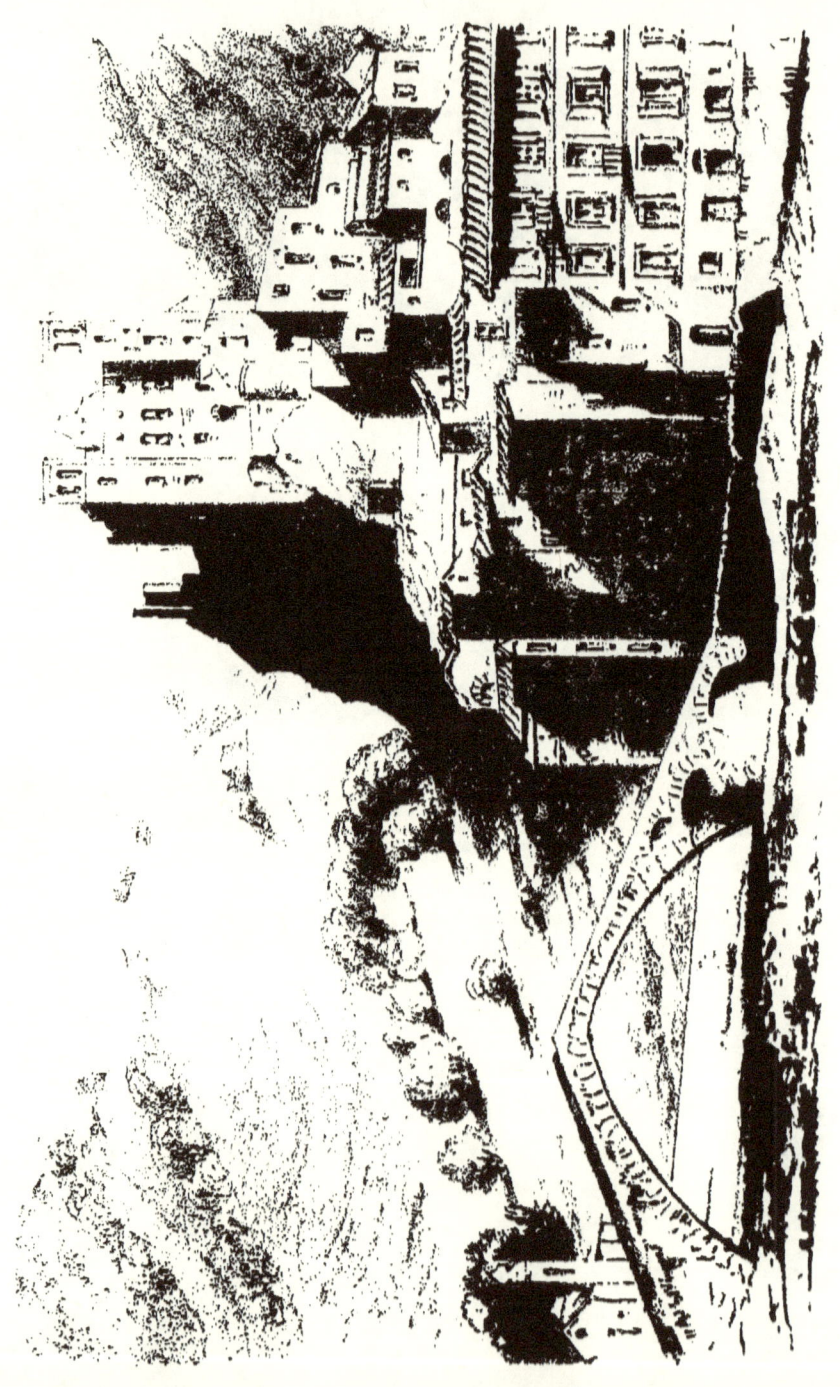

VENTIMIGLIA, BORDIGHERA, AND DOLCEACQUA.

Jan. 26.

WE have now been several times to Ventimiglia, which is five miles from hence, a beautiful drive along the Genoa Cornice. At the little half-way village of St. Mauro, whose painted church rises on an olive-clad promontory against the blue sea, is the Sardinian custom house, where carriages from Mentone draw up for an instant, but are allowed to go on without further hindrance when the driver calls out "c'est une promenade." The whole of the latter part of the way, the fine castle of Ventimiglia, which forms the chief fortress between Genoa and Nice, rises before you, crowning the brown precipices with its white walls.

The fortress is entered by gates and a drawbridge, closing the narrow passage of the rocky steep, which could be easily guarded and will remind the traveller in Southern Italy of the pass at Terracina. Within, the town runs along a ledge of rock in a picturesque outline of brightly coloured towers, old houses, and deserted convents, while below lies a little port with fishing vessels and some curiously pointed isolated rocks.

La Strada Grande is narrow and quaint, lined with fine old houses, some of which are painted on the outside with figures of animals, while others retain in marble balconies, relics of their former grandeur. People talk Italian, and women shout, as at Naples, before the stalls of maccaroni and pollenta, in the dark archways. The Cathedral, of which St. Barnabas is said to have been the first bishop, is a long picturesque building, with a curious apse, a grey Lombardo-gothic porch, and a tall tower. Beside it stands the huge palace of the Lascaris, with an open loggia and staircase, reminding one of mediæval pictures of the death of John the Baptist, in which Herodias' daughter looks over a balcony at the top of the broad twisted stairs, on which servants are walking to and fro with dishes for the feast, while the execution is going on beneath.

A beautiful subject for a drawing is afforded by the east end of the Cathedral, where the bright colouring of the building contrasts well with the grand background of snow mountains, beyond the broad stony bed of the torrent Roya. But the finest view of all is from beneath, in the bed of the torrent itself, whence the town is seen rising gradually in tier above tier of old houses, churches and convents, with purple mountains and snow peaks beyond, and in the foreground the long bridge of irregular pointed arches, occasionally replaced by timber, while groups of gaily-dressed washerwomen are at work upon the sand-banks in the bed of the river.

A path, which turns aside to the left from the bridge, leads through a low postern gate to a narrow staircase up the inside of the city walls, and overhanging the orange-gardens at a considerable height. No one is advised to try it, who is not tolerably steady of head, and sure of foot, though it is the nearest way to St. Michaele, a yellow brown Romanesque church on the crest of the hill. This church is worthy of attentive observation; the rough stone walls of the interior remain in their original state, and the crypt is a remarkably fine one. St. Michaele was first a temple of Castor and Pollux, and afterwards a Benedictine Convent. The view from below this church is one of the most striking on the whole Riviera. Two Roman mile-stones are preserved here, one bearing the number DXC, and inscriptions of Augustus and Antoninus Pius. The church tower and village which rise from the moist meadows and olive groves beyond the bridge, belong to the Borgo di Ventimiglia, which contains many quaint bits of architecture, and where there is a pleasant little inn, called the Albergo della Scatola. Here luncheon may be obtained, and eaten on the flat balustraded roof, whence there is a lovely view of the town, with its old houses, and its castle cresting the opposite hill.

An inn at Ventimiglia, was, about the year 1850, the scene of a romantic incident in the life of Francesco Novello di Carrara, Lord of Padua, whose history is pleasantly told by "the author of Mary Powell" in her "Story of Italy." It happened when Francesco was flying for his life from his hereditary enemy, the Count di Virtù, with his wife, his two brothers, and three servants. "After a long and fatiguing journey on foot, they stopped at an inn near Ventimiglia for refreshment; and a man, struck with the singularity of their appearance, hastened to tell the podestà that six men with a lady of incomparable beauty, and apparently of high rank, were refreshing themselves at an inn near the gates, and that the lady was doubtless being carried off against her will."

This romantic story caused the podesta to send a guard of soldiers after them. Meanwhile, the Signor and the lady, who was '*bella, bella veramente,*' were resuming their way, when, hearing the regular tramp of soldiers' feet, they hastily plunged into a thicket. They were pursued and overtaken, but so close to the shore, that Francesco fought his way to the boat, and defended himself till all but he were in it.

Then he was overpowered and captured at the water's very edge. The principal boatman cried out in alarm, 'Have a care what you do. He is the Signor Francesco di Carrara, Lord of Padua.' 'Ah, my lord, then said the leader of the soldiers, we knew not it was you; but thought you were carrying off that lady against her will.'

Francesco, finding the harmless nature of the mistake, willingly went to the podesta and explained it to him; and the podesta with great kindness sent a fresh supply of provisions to his vessel, to which the Signor then returned."

It requires many visits to explore Ventimiglia thoroughly; it has such endless beauty in its decayed archways, painted walls, and moss-grown fountains, to say nothing of the purple hills which surround it, and the everlasting snows upon which it looks out. It has now regained the position of frontier town of the kingdom of Piedmont, which it occupied before the union of Piedmont with Mentone and Roccabruna at the revolution. In its early existence it bore the name of Albium Intermelium, and was the capital of the Intermelians, a Ligurian tribe. In the middle ages, while its fortress was held by the great family of Lascaris, its possession was constantly disputed in turn by the Genoese, the Counts of Provence, and the Dukes of Savoy. Monks and priests of every description still flourish and abound in it.

Bordighera is separated from Ventimiglia by about three miles of flat and dusty level, which seems like one continuous suburb, from the number of country houses which line it. The river Nervia is crossed by a handsome stone bridge of three arches, approached by a causeway. Hence is a fine view of the snow mountains up its valley, in which is situated the ruined castle of Dolceacqua. Groups of palm trees appear gradually by the road side, and increase on approaching Bordighera. This place, which has been surnamed "the Jericho of Italy," was almost unknown in England till a few years ago, has now become familiar through Signor Ruffini's beautiful story of Doctor Antonio, in which the principal scene is laid here. The story is in fact subordinate to the descriptions, whose accuracy will be appreciated by those who visit the place itself, which, though not one of the most beautiful on the coast, is thoroughly Italian in all its characteristics. The town contains nothing worth visiting, so that it is best to leave the carriage in the street and to wander up the hill, first to the garden of the French consul, where are some of the finest palm trees, mingled with beautiful flowers; and from hence, passing through the town, the stranger should wander over the common at the hill top, the view from which is best described by the following quotation from Doctor Antonio :—

"A glorious extent of hilly coast against a back ground of lofty mountains, stretched semicircularly from east to west, broken all along into capes and creeks, and studded with towns and villages, full of original character,—Ventimiglia with its crown of dismantled mediæval castles,— Mentone, so gay on its sunny beach,—well-named Roccabruna, all sombre hues and frowns,—Turbia, and its Roman monument, a record of the greatest power on earth, covering with its shadow the lilliputian principality of Monaco below,—Villafranca and its lighthouse.

"Further on, running southward, looms vaporous in the distance, the long low strip of French shore, with Antibes in the extremity; and further still, in the west, the fanciful blue lines of the mountains of Provence. Here and there a snowy peak shoots boldly above the rest; some hoary parent Alp, one might fancy, looking down to see that all goes right among the younger branches."

From this common a winding path descends again to the shore at the point of the rocky bay, which is the scene of another of Ruffini's descriptions.

"It is indeed a beauteous scene. In front lies the immensity of sea, smooth as glass, and rich with all the hues of a dove's neck, the bright green, the dark purple, the soft ultramarine, the deep blue of a blade of burnished steel,—there glancing in the sun like diamonds, and rippling into a lace-like net of snowy foam. In strong relief against this bright background, stands a group of red-capped, red-belted fishermen, drawing their nets to the shore, and accompanying each pull with a plaintive burden, that the echo of the mountains sends softened back. On the right to the westward, the silvery track of the road undulating amid thinly scattered houses, or clusters of orange and palm trees, leads the eye to the promontory of Bordighera, a huge emerald mound which shuts out the horizon, much in the shape of a leviathan couchant, his broad muzzle buried in the waters. Here you have in a small compass, refreshing to behold, every shade of green that can gladden the eye, from the pale grey olive to the dark foliaged cypress, of which one, ever and anon, an isolated sentinel, shoots forth high above the rest. Tufts of feathery palms, their heads tipped by the sun, the lower part in shade, spread their broad branches, like warriors' crests on the top, where the slender *silhouette* of the towering church spire cuts sharply against the spotless sky."

The coast to the east recedes inland with a graceful curve, then with a gentle bend to the south is lost by degrees in the far, far sea. Three headlands arise from this cresent, which so lovingly receives to its embrace a wide expanse of the weary waters; three headlands of differing aspect and colour, lying one behind the other. The nearest is a bare red rock, so fiery in the sun the eye dares scarcely rest on it; the second, richly wooded, wears on its loftiest ridge a long hamlet, like to a mural crown; the third looks a mere blue mist in the distance, save one white speck. Two bright sails are rounding this last cape. The whole, flooded as it is with light, except where some projecting crag casts its transparent grey shadow, is seen again reversed, and in more faint loveliness, in the watery mirror below. Earth, sea, and sky mingle their different tones, and from their varieties, as from the notes of a rich, full chord, rises one great harmony. Golden atoms are floating in the translucent air, and a halo of mother-of-pearl colour hangs over the sharp outlines of the mountains.

The small village at the foot of the craggy mountain is called Spedaletti, and gives its name to the gulf. It means little hospitals, and is supposed to have originated in a ship belonging to the knights of Rhodes having landed some men sick of the plague here, where barracks were erected for their reception; and these same buildings, served as the first nucleus of the present village, which has naturally retained the name of their first destination. At a little distance are the ruins of a chapel called the "Ruota," which may or may not be a corruption of Rodi (Rhodes). Spedaletti in the present day is exclusively inhabited by the wealthy families of very industrious fishermen, who need never be in want of occupation. Nature, which made this bay so lovely, made it equally safe and trustworthy. Sheltered on the west by the Cape of Bordighera, and on the east by those three headlands, let the sea be ever so high without, within it is comparatively calm, and the fishermen of Spedaletti are out in all weathers.

The village perched so boldly on the brow of the second mountain, just above Spedaletti, is appropriately called La Colla (the hill). It is interesting to know that while the cholera was raging fearfully at San Remo, which lies at the foot of the other side of the mountain, not one case was heard of at La Colla. Its extremely elevated situation accounts very well for its escape. But a more striking and really explicable fact is that the fatal scourge did not get round that second cape, the cape of San Remo, but leaped at once to Nice, sparing all the intermediate tract of country. The white speck gleaming out so brightly on the far-away promontory is another sanctuary, the Madonna *della Guardia,* a would-be rival of that of Lampedusa, but beaten hollow by the latter.

Palms are so common at Bordighera, that all the little children were picking and eating the unripe dates as they pleased, and were playing with long white palm branches which a Roman martyr might have envied—literally " strewing palm branches in the way." When they were tired they came and sat down by us and sang in chorus one of the " canzoni popolari " of the present day, the burden of which was, of course, " Viva Vittorio et viva Garibaldi."

There are frightful precipices on the way to Ventimiglia, as we have reason to know, from an adventure which befell us in returning from thence. Our coachman would drive us so near the edge of the precipices, and urge on his three horses so fast, that from the first it was very alarming. We were just congratulating ourselves upon having a very low wall at the side of the road, which gave us at least a slight protection, while before we had had none, when there was a frightful tustle among the horses, who seemed suddenly to veer round and make for the edge; the fact being that the outside horse had got his leg over the shaft, and was pushing the others. Thinking that anything would be preferable to being dashed to pieces in the abyss beneath, I threw myself out, and when I looked up unhurt, all three horses were hanging over the edge and looking like a network of legs, as they were caught together on a ledge whence a solitary olive tree sprung out of the rock, and which alone prevented them from rolling into the sea; the carriage, with its broken shafts sticking straight up into the air, was tottering on the verge of the precipice, but was prevented from quite going over by the broken fragment of wall into which it was jammed. My companions were still sitting in it, but the driver and courier had thrown themselves off on the first alarm.

A number of people soon collected, but all were too much frightened to be of much use, and it was with difficulty that a man could be persuaded to help in pushing back the broken carriage, and a woman to help to hold the horses, as they were successively dragged up, quivering with terror. Strange to say, none of them were much hurt, though from the extreme narrowness of the place on which they were caught, it was very difficult to disentangle them. The carriage was left to be mended, and the horses to be healed, and we walked on.

The night was cold and the wind bitter. As we drew near St. Mauro, we seemed likely to come in for a second adventure, for the dark sky became suddenly illuminated, and the blaze was so great, that we imagined the whole village must be in flames. The picturesque old church, with its painted tower, stood out quite golden and brilliant against the deep black-blue of the sky; beneath, Rembrandt-like figures in long cloaks passed to and fro in the red fire-light, and when, as if in a play, loud and repeated explosions were added to the gorgeous wreaths of coloured smoke and flame above, and the flickering glow on the olive trees below, the effect was most extraordinary. We were in the height of our amazement, when we remembered that the next day was sacred to St. Mauro, and that these fiery festivities must be celebrating the eve of his fête.

On the rugged precipices above the Pont St. Louis, the carriage came up to us, with two of its horses, having been mended at Ventimiglia, where the third horse had been left behind to recruit. One of our companions was so tired, that, on the assurances of the driver and courier that all was now safe, we got in again, though not without many misgivings. They were not uncalled for; before we had gone many yards, the outside horse again put his leg over the pole, and again forced the other towards the precipice. I once more threw myself out upon the road, and on the driver's screaming " Sortez, sortez," the others followed. But, seeing nothing else could save the carriage from going over this time, the driver, by a sudden jerk, threw down his horses on the road, who thus served as a lock to the carriage, which rolled upon them, on the steep incline. After this second escape, it may be imagined, that we walked the rest of the way home.

On the following day (Jan. 15) we returned to St. Mauro for the fête, going on donkeys as far as the steep little narrow path which winds up into the village. A crowd of peasants, in holiday costume, were collected on the platform in front of the gaily-painted little church, where music and litanies were going on. At each side were booths filled with sweetmeats, toffy stuffed with almonds, little images in paste of St. Mauro, curious little musical instruments at ten soldi a-piece, and pairs of the national earrings at four. One stall also was piled with books, most of which contained sacred dramas—"The Prodigal Son paraphrased," or scenes in which the dramatis personæ were Mary and Martha, Mary Magdalene and Santa Maria Salome. For two soldi we also obtained the "Vita del glorioso San Giosafat," with a portrait of that saint in a long garment of his own uncombed hair, and the "Piacevole e ridicolosa semplicita di Bertoldino.'

At 4 p.m. the peasants began to dance before the church.

Yesterday (Jan. 25), there was a very pretty festa at the tiny church of St. Agostino, which is situated in a wooded glen half-way between St. Mauro and Ventimiglia, with snowy mountains seen gleaming through its trees. The church itself is quite a little gem of the kind, and is brilliantly painted all over. Above the door is inscribed—

> "CHINI LA TESTA ALTIERA,
> IL PECCATOR SERONTATO
> QUI PORGA UMIL PREGHIERA
> AL SUO SIGNORE IRATO." 1799.

and two little cherubs holding scrolls, inscribed, "Amare quod credidit," and "Predicare quod docuit."

Two marble pillars in the interior appear to be relics of an older church. The village near this is named "Latte" (the Land of Milk) from the richness of its soil, though a village it can scarcely be called, as it consists of a series of campagnes near the sea-shore, (among which, the largest is the summer palace of the bishops of Ventimiglia,) and of a machicolated mediæval tower in a vineyard. This is the scene so admirably described by Mrs. Gretton in her "Englishwoman in Italy," as the place where she visited the Comtesse de Laval.

Those who intend to visit Dolceacqua, must leave their carriages on this side of the river Nervia, which is crossed by the road, half-way between Ventimiglia and Bordighera, and follow the mule path which ascends its left bank. This path sometimes descending to the stony bed of the river, sometimes overhanging it, and fringed with rosemary and myrtle, has a view all the way of the town of Campo-Rosso, nestling in the depth of the valley, with a chain of lofty snow-peaks behind it. Drawing nearer, Campo-Rosso is found to be one of the most picturesque towns in the whole district; first comes a brown conventual church, with a painted campanile, relieved against the purple distance, and then you enter the town which surrounds a piazza, lined with the quaintest old houses, with open painted loggias, and ending in a curious church, whose staircase of white marble is flanked by two marble mermaids, throwing water into two small fountains. The number of brown monks, looking down from latticed upper windows, or meandering about under the painted archways, add much to the character of the place. A little further, on the right of the road, is an old Romanesque church, containing a very early illuminated altar, and possessing a burial ground, near the banks of the Nervia, overgrown with periwinkles, and shaded by tall cypresses. An inscription entreats "elemōsina" for the "Anime Purganti," and the former possessors of the "Anime" are represented by a pile of skulls and skeletons mouldering together in an open charnel-house.

After two miles more of lanes, winding through woods of olives, carpeted by young corn and bright green flax, Dolceacqua suddenly bursts upon the view stretching across a valley, whose sides are covered with forests of olives and chesnuts, and which is backed by fine snow-mountains. Through the town winds the deep blue stream of the Nervia, flowing under a tall bridge, which is like the Rialto of Venice, in its great span and height, and above frowns the huge palatial castle of the Dorias, perched upon a perpendicular cliff, with sunlight streaming through its long lines of glassless windows. The streets, like those of St. Remo, are almost closed in with archways, which give them the appearance of exaggerated crypts, only opening here and there to let in a ray of sunlight, and a strip of blue sky. They lead up the steep ascent to the castle, where the immense ruined halls of the sovereign princes of Dolceacqua, are now only paved with fresh green turf, enamelled with flowers. All who visit it must unite in thinking that Dolceacqua is the most beautiful, as Peglione is the wildest scene in the neighbourhood.

It is a walk of about three-and-a-half miles to Dolceacqua after leaving the carriage at the bridge over the Nervia, and this may be accomplished without fatigue, by writing beforehand to engage donkeys at Ventimiglia. The road after leaving Campo-Rosso is excellent, and the whole might easily be accomplished in a carriage, if the Nervia had not washed away a short portion of the road, between the bridge and Campo-Rosso.

TURBIA, LAGHETTO, AND ESA.

Jan. 31.

ONE of our latest excursions has been to Turbia, about eight miles in the direction of Nice. It rained furiously, but we are beginning to learn that the country is quite as striking and beautiful in wet weather as in fine, and Turbia looked magnificent, amidst the driving storm-clouds, which opened to reveal the view of the bays of Mentone on one side, and of Villafranca on the other. Above a nest of little brown houses rises the huge ruin of the Trophœa Augusti, and though the church and village are both built out of its materials, the remaining half of the solid round tower, is still a gigantic mass, defying storm and time.

This building, from which the name of Turbia (Trophæa) had its origin, was raised by the emperor Augustus, after his conquest of the various Alpine tribes, and was placed by him on the most conspicuous point of the Maritime Alps, on the spot which is indicated in the itinerary of Antoninus as "Alpis Summa." After the barbarian invasion the monument was partly destroyed, and served to form a tower, of which only a portion still stands; the present remains being those of the debris of a great Roman work of an early period, forming the base of another tower erected during the middle ages. Huge stones are strewn

ESA.

around, hewn from a neighbouring height, where one may still perceive the traces of Roman work; and pieces of marble, which must once have belonged to the ancient monument, are scattered over the walls of the village and church. The mediæval tower remained entire till the year 1706, when, being considered as a fortification, it was destroyed by the mines of the French army, at the same time with the castle of Nice. The ruins still shew the traces of fire.

The primitive monument was also destroyed by fire, of which the marks were visible in the 15th century, when it was described by Pierre Antoine Boyer, a Franciscan monk. The original base is described as square; 230 feet in breadth, upon which stood another square of finer workmanship, and ten feet smaller, while the top of the monument was round, 800 feet in circuit, and ornamented by columns. The whole was crowned by a colossal statue of Augustus. Gioffredi mentions, that beneath a picture of St. Honorius, in his island near Cannes, there existed an ancient inscription, which stated that the fall of the statue was owing to the prayers of that saint, on account of its having become an object of idolatry, and he adds that a picture representing this miracle was to be seen in the church of St. Dominic at Nice. The Pere Boyer also speaks of two sarcophagi, formed from parts of the statue after its fall, which existed in his time in the church of La Turbia; one of these is stated by the old inhabitants to have been used in building the new church, just before the revolution, the other still exists outside the church, and though much injured, shews part of a human body in the carving of one of its sides, which may have formed a portion of the famous statue.

Among the marbles found here was a fine head of Drusus,

which was bought by the Prince of Denmark, and is now in the museum at Copenhagen. The Roman road "Julia Augusta," (also called the Emilian Way, from Emilius Scaurus, under whose auspices this part of the road was formed,) passed in front of the monument. Hence the Roman way descended to the valley by the ravine of Laghetto, on the western side of which are some inscribed Roman mile-stones, regarded with great reverence by the peasants, who imagine that the "Written Rocks" (Pietre Scrittē) must have been the work of magical hands.

The precipices prevent the drive to Turbia being a pleasant one in the Mentonese carriages, which are constantly having accidents, but we took courage to face them a second time, in order to make a pilgrimage to the Madonna di Laghetto, which indeed it was only our duty to do, according to the national custom for all those who have escaped from a carriage accident in the Riviera. Only people were rather shocked, that we had no ex-voto, to take with us as an offering.

A little beyond Turbia, we turned off to the right, at a place which has the title of Santa Caterina, a name which the natives assert was derived from its chapel, an edifice which at first we believed to be mythical, but at length we discovered its remains in a low ruined wall, still retaining some faded frescoes of St. Catherine and other virgin saints. Near it stands the "Colonna del Ré," commemorating the pilgrimage of King Charles Felix, for which the present road to the convent was constructed in 1826. Hence the road plunges into an arid and stony valley, devoid alike of vegetation and feature, till at length it suddenly opens, to display a range of wild mountains, ending in the grand snow-peaks which close the valley of the Var.

Here, at the foot of Mount Sembola, perched on a rugged rock, stands the convent, isolated in wet weather by the mountain torrents which surround it on every side, and then unite again, to fall into the Paillon far below in the plain.

The building is most picturesque. The tall painted tower of the church, capped by its quaint dome, rises above the other monastic buildings, which are grouped together with much variety of colour in their yellow walls, red roofs, and bright green jalousies, casting long shadows in the sunshine. A few grey aloes with their immense prickly leaves, and some very old olive trees, vary the uniformity of the rock, while two or three large umbrella pines, on the edge of the rift above the little village of Laghetto, form a good foreground to the rugged mountain range which closes in the valley on its three sides. A fine modern bridge, with an older one in ruins below, allows the road to pass to the sanctuary across the ravine of Perdiguierre, which runs below it.

Near this, Monsieur Ciotti, a late Intendant-General of Nice, who made the road, and built the bridge, has also erected a stable for the accommodation of visitors. The paved piazza in the front of the convent, as well as the road and the bridge, are generally filled with brown cowled monks, strolling about or playing at bowls in the sun. The entrance to the convent is by a broad open cloister, where pilgrims go through their novenas before entering the church, and where the walls are covered with ex-votos.

Among these, the pictures of horrible scenes placed there to commemorate the various accidents that had taken place, made our fright at Ventimiglia dwindle into nothing in comparison. Here were horses backing their carriages over awful precipices; there, the horses themselves plunging over the edge of the abyss, and perfect showers of unfortunate travellers raining out of the carriages into the gulf below. Some of the pictures evidently represented adventures which had occurred to visitors going to Laghetto itself, the convent and the monks being displayed in the background. The shipwreck scenes were also most terrific.

In the centre of the cloister, which was entirely built by the offerings of the faithful, is the church (restored in 1838), which is small, but well proportioned, lofty and handsome, with two side chapels, dedicated to St. Joseph and St. Theresa. The whole is painted in imitation of marble, and is covered with ex-votos of a superior kind. These include silver hearts, bridal wreaths, and the crutches offered by the lame. The altar was formerly laden with precious chandeliers and lamps, which were always kept burning in honour of the Virgin, but at the time of the French invasion, *the exigencies of the State* required that these should be carried to Turin. Above the altar, however, still remains the famous statue of the Virgin and Child, which is shown by the sacristan if called for.

It is a ruddy looking image, dressed in a cloak, embroidered with gold and silver, and holding in its hand a scapular; the device which the Virgin is said to have brought herself from heaven, and presented to the order of the Carmelites, as a special mark of her favour. The golden crowns on her head and that of her child, are enriched with precious stones, which were presented by the Contessa Riccardi of Oneglia. On high festivals, but especially those of Pentecost, St. Peter, St. Paul, Notre Dame de Carmel, Sta. Theresa, and the Holy Trinity, almost the whole native population of Nice, and the surrounding villages, flows up to this remote mountain to visit and adore the image. On the Holy Trinity the immense number of pilgrims make the cloisters and their surrounding valleys echo incessantly to their hymns to the glory of Mary. Tents are pitched on the platform of the convent, where hundreds who come from the more distant places, bivouack through the night, or even spend many days, sleeping in tents, living in the open air, and feeding on the provisions they have brought with them. A number of sick or crippled persons are carried in the processions, bearing rich gifts as propitiatory offerings. These usually arrive at the convent in the evening, and spend the night in preparation in the church itself, "some make the air resound with the praises of the Virgin, others weep and confess their sins at the feet of the monks. In the morning the sacrament is administered, followed by a sermon on the virtues of Mary, and on the cordial confidence which ought to be placed in her prompt and powerful succour in every time of need." After this the sick prostrate themselves at the feet of the image. When this moment arrives, a wild fervour seizes every one, and unanimous cries of "Grace, Grace, Marie" are uttered by every lip, tears stream from all eyes, and the emotion becomes universal. Then—

"Les dons, les ex-votos, les offrandes s'accrurent,
　Aveugles, sourds, blessés, malades accoururent,
　　Et l'on vit s'accomplir nombre de guérisons.
　Les rois mêmes, courbant leurs fronts et leurs couronnes
　Vinrent soliciter au profit de leurs trônes.
　　Pour leurs peuples, pour leurs maisons."

The statue of the Virgin, although fresh with paint and

K

gilding, dates from the 16th century, and occupies the place of a far older image, which is said still to exist in the neighbourhood, though it is not shown.

The original image, according to local tradition and the papers of the Fenogli family of Ventimiglia, was discovered by a young man of that town, who went to visit his sister at Turbia. While staying with her, he went out shooting in the neighbourhood. When he reached the hill of Laghetto, not far from an old wall, upon which, in a kind of niche, was a painted figure of the Virgin, he saw a bird nestling among the leaves of the brambles, and shot it dead. But on coming nearer, he was seized with a religious terror, on observing that the ball had struck the Virgin on the breast, whence blood was issuing. Believing that he had unintentionally committed a sacrilege, he hurried back to his family, and related his strange adventure, upon which they decided to build an expiatory chapel on that very spot.

In 1652, when nothing remained of this chapel except the wooden statue, worm eaten and nearly split in two by age, Hyacinthe Casanova, a native of Monaco, who believed that his recovery from a dangerous illness was due to the intercession of the Virgin, first urged the erection of the present chapel, to which the image which is now shown, was presented by Antonio Fighiera, a lawyer of Nice, in whose family it had long been venerated. From this time the reputed miracles of Laghetto increased to such a degree, that in 1633, even the Bishop of Nice refused to believe in them, and caused the church to be shut up; but after a public examination he was induced to reopen it, when the image underwent a solemn coronation, the town of Nice at the same time choosing the Madonna of Laghetto as its special patroness and protectress. A road was then made to render the image more accessible to pilgrims, and a convent was built for Carmelite monks to guard the shrine, and to sing night and day the praises of " the mother of God." The princes and princesses of Savoy have always been indefatigable in their pilgrimages to Laghetto, especially King Charles Emmanuel II, who reigned in 1652, and who, having placed his sick child under the protection of this particular image, presented it, when the child recovered, with a golden baby of the size and weight of his own. This, with all the other treasures of the shrine, was carried off in 1792 by the French, who plundered and destroyed everything except the image itself, which had been smuggled away to La Turbia before their arrival. It remained there till 1802, when it was brought back in a grand procession with immense pomp.

In front of the convent are two interesting inscriptions; one is upon the pedestal of the fountain, and may be thus translated :—

" Pilgrim, you find here two streams, one descends from heaven, the other from the top of the mountains. The first is a treasure which the Virgin distributes to the piety of the faithful, the second has been brought here by the people of Nice; drink of both, if you thirst for both." A.D. 1654.

The other inscription commemorates an extraordinary and grand scene in Italian history, to which Laghetto has been witness, and which ought to render it far more celebrated than either the image or its reputed miracles. It was in this lonely valley, among these desolate mountains, that King Charles Albert, the beloved of his people, determining to preserve his honour and keep his faith, even by the sacrifice of his kingdom, took leave of his court, his crown, and the world.

QUI,
LA MATTINA DEL 26 MARZO 1849,
CARLO ALBERTO
LASCIATI I CAMPI FATALI DI NOVARA
SOSTAVA IGNOTO ESULANTE.

QUI
PIAMENTE CONFESSÒ, E ALLA MENSA DI GESÙ
RICONFORTATO LO SPIRITO AFFRANTO
RINOVÒ IL SACRIFIZIO DI AFFETTI E DI DOLORI.

QUI
PERDONO L'INJURIE
PIANSE LE COMMUNE SCIAGURE
E ABBANDONANDO COLLA PRESENZA L'ITALIA
NE RACCOMANDAVA I DESTINI
AL PATROCINIO DELLA VERGINE MADRE.

HERE,
ON THE MORNING OF THE 26TH OF MARCH 1849,
CHARLES ALBERT
AFTER LEAVING THE FATAL FIELD OF NOVARA
STOPT, AN UNKNOWN EXILE.

HERE,
HAVING DEVOUTLY CONFESSED, AND AT THE TABLE OF JESUS
REFRESHED HIS WEARY SPIRIT,
HE RENEWED THE SACRIFICE OF HIS AFFECTIONS AND SORROWS.

HERE,
HE FORGAVE HIS INJURIES
HE GRIEVED FOR THE COMMON DISASTERS;
AND ABANDONING ITALY IN PERSON,
HE RECOMMENDED ITS DESTINIES
TO THE PATRONAGE OF THE VIRGIN MOTHER.

No one should leave Laghetto without descending the valley for a short distance, for by far the finest view of the convent is from below, whence it appears rising abruptly from a bold grey rock half buried in dark ilex woods, and backed by purple mountains. Another fine point of view, may be obtained from the winding path above the convent, with the two bridges in its foreground. The monks sell medals, with pictures of the shrine, a short history of the place, and an "Ode historique à Notre Dame de Laghet."

The name Laghetto is derived from the fact that once when the torrent was unusually swollen by the melting of the mountain snows, the fall of a large rock so effectually checked its progress to the sea, that the whole valley became a lake.

Two miles beyond Turbia, the Saracenic town of Esa is seen against the sea, perched on a rugged crag; its situation is one of the most striking on the Riviera, and is wild and picturesque in the extreme.

This fortress was used by the pirates, who formerly infested this coast, as one of their chief strongholds, for which its isolated position and tremendous precipices gave it a natural fitness. It is approached by a path which descends the ravine from the road to Nice, and then winds up through the olive terraces beyond, or on the side towards Nice, by the "Anse d'Esa," and a staircase cut in the face of the cliff.

There is a path hence by the sea-shore to Monaco, through very grand scenery, and beneath gigantic cliffs.

IL GRAN' MONDO.

Feb. 1.

ABOVE the olive-clad hills on the east of Mentone, rises a bare mountain peak, of micacious limestone, which gleams white against the blue sky on a sunshiny morning. This mountain, known as the Berceau, is one of the favorite expeditions from Mentone, being the nearest point whence the map-like appearance of the different valleys, and the grand chain of snowy Alps, can be seen at once, and being easily manageable in a day's excursion.

The road thither passes through Castellare, and it is well for those who wish to save themselves fatigue, to take donkeys thus far, and indeed as much further as possible, for the last part of the way is very steep and impracticable, except for walkers. The view from the Berceau is very fine, and the snow Alps are seen from thence rising above the nearer hills, but it is not to be compared to that from a more distant mountain generally known by its patois name of Gran' Mondo, which intercepts what would otherwise be the finest part of the view from the Berceau.

We made a party for this expedition last Monday, and at eight o'clock were climbing, some on donkeys, some on foot, up the tufa staircase, and through the steep pine woods to Castellare. Here, in the narrow street, where the golden sunlight was just breaking in upon the gloom of the dirty old houses, the usual morning smells saluted us. The path in the bare mountain beyond, is overhung by the Saracenic fortress, and the jagged walls of old Castellare, half overgrown with ivy, and standing thirteen hundred and fifty feet above the sea. This stronghold, which was a terror to the middle ages, became still more so during the French revolution, when band after band of emigrés, attempting to escape into Sardinia by its solitary pass, were taken and murdered by its covetous inhabitants. Hence some of the walkers in our party diverged to the Berceau. At this point also, our donkeys, which had been getting on very badly for some time, collapsed altogether, and giving vent to horrible inward heavings, looked so like dying, that we were obliged to leave them, to return to Castellare when sufficiently recovered, and wait for us there till the evening. It was evident that they had nothing to eat that day, and were sinking from faintness and starvation; the moral of which is, to insist upon the Theresines feeding them well before setting out upon any long expedition. Beyond this point the way is difficult to find, so, on reaching a brown desolate chapel on the ridge of the mountain, we persuaded a little peasant to go with us as guide, he, declaring he knew the way, and his father directing him to take us without fail, "Alla cima stessa del Gran' Mondo." However, the sultriness of the day, and the incessant ups and downs by which he led us, made us all very impatient, and we had not gone far before two of our party began to doubt both his knowledge and his veracity, and on his sturdily persisting that his way was the right one, they deserted us and went off in another direction. We continued to follow a desolate valley between high mountains, till the path became very intricate, and at length the boy, bursting into floods of tears, cried out in piteous patois, "Non c'è strada più, non so la strada, non so niente." There was certainly an end of the way, and above us towered the barren peak of the Gran' Mondo, seemingly an inaccessible precipice. The view, however, was very beautiful, of the snowy range, rising from deep purple rocks, over which cloud shadows were calmly floating, while a huge cliff, jagged in outline, and varied in colour, divided the picture in half. It was really almost too hot in the glowing February sun, though snow lay thick around in the hollow of the rock, and the dips in the stunted yellow turf. Two of us sat down to draw, and when we had finished, all our companions were gone leaving no sign left to tell what had become of them. However, we determined to go on, and find the best way we could to the summit. So up we toiled, sometimes slipping down on our faces in the snow, sometimes crawling on our hands and knees in the rough beds of slippery shale, which came roaring down with our weight, as if the whole mountain was coming down upon us. At last we reached the top, with its cluster of huge boulder stones, which are wonderously heaped together at the very "cima del monte," and had the comfort of knowing we were a good deal higher than everything else we saw, except the eternal snows themselves. The view is magnificent; on the north, across a gulf of green pines, is the glorious line of snowy peaks, with their purple children beneath; on the east a ruin, perhaps of a Saracenic stronghold, crowning a neighbouring crag, and below, the stony bed of the Roya winding away to Ventimiglia; on the west, swelling blue mountains, among which rises the castellated rock of St. Agnese; and on the south, amid rolling clouds, the Berceau, black in the afternoon shadow, and above it the vast expanse of the Mediterranean, beyond the horizon of which, as we stood watching, one after another of the snowy peaks of Corsica, slowly revealed themselves. Among the rocks grew a number of small auricula and saxifrage plants; and when we had dug up as many of these as we could carry, it was time to descend.

We thought we should be too late to go along the ridge to the Berceau, though that way is quite practicable, and not at all dangerous earlier in the day, and we were so afraid of finding ourselves at Ventimiglia, whither all the other paths lead, that we decided it would be best to go down the same way by which we had come up. Rocks, however, and stones, are singularly alike on the Gran' Mondo, and somehow we missed our track, and found ourselves in worse beds of sliding shale than ever. "It won't do, I do not think it will do," was the constant cry of my companion, but a roar of stones falling under hurrying feet was his only answer, for the mist was rising so fast, that there was no time to be lost, as the Gran' Mondo would soon be enveloped, and then we might be anywhere, probably in the bed of the Roya itself, before we knew how to help ourselves.

When we had reached the bottom of the first descent, we left the mist behind us, and the view was again clear, hill and river and valley lying below us like a map, yet all seemed strange. "Can you recognise any single object you have ever seen before in your life," said my companion. "No," I was forced to answer, "not one single object." We had evidently lost our way. In this position the only thing which seemed clear was, that if we kept to the valleys, we could not fall over precipices and on this we acted, and hurried downwards incessantly and as quickly as we could; at last, after incessant jumping from one rock terrace to another, we descried a tiny path, but evidently utterly unfrequented, for a goatherd, who appeared like a vision against the sky, on a mountain peak above our heads, held up his hands in astonishment, at the sight of two Englishmen in that desert place, while he shrieked at us in patois. At last we regained a path which, after some hard walking, led us out close to the deserted chapel, where we had first engaged our guide, and near this we picked up three of our party, who had also arrived by another way at the summit of the Gran' Mondo, where they had refreshed themselves with sherry iced in snow, and had come down again without losing themselves. The rest were not so fortunate. The last objects we saw were the two first deserters who had wandered on to the Berceau, shouting at the top of an inaccessible precipice above old Castellare, where they were overtaken by the mist, and were near being kept till morning. The party who had gone originally to the Berceau lost their way altogether, and one lady falling down and spraining her ankle severely, had to be dragged along by her companions, during their wanderings among rocks and olive woods, and down the beds of torrents, till at last they emerged more dead than alive, close to the cemetery of Mentone.

On the way down to Castellare, we met with one more adventure. Half-way down the narrow precipitous path, we heard a noise behind us, and on looking round, saw a runaway mule, which seemed to have been driven mad by overdriving and beating, and which was rushing down the mountain, with red glaring eyes, and uttering the dreadful peculiar cry, which only an angry mule knows how to make. It was rushing straight at us, and there was only just time to jump upon the olive terrace below, before the furious beast arrived, and stood raging on the path above, and trying all it could to get down after us. Happily we had two white umbrellas, and by poking them in its face, we contrived to keep it at bay, till its owners, who were running down the mountain after it, came to the rescue.

Twilight fell as we entered Castellare, where we were refreshed by some wine in the "Piazza Grande," and where we found our donkeys waiting for us, who, we were glad to discover had a much better knowledge of the way than we had ourselves, for it was pitch dark when we reached Mentone, and the descent into its narrow lanes between high walls, was like going down into Hades.

One of the ladies of our party went to a ball in the evening, and was looked upon as quite a heroine by the Mentonese. "No lady," they said, "at Mentone, had ever been up the Gran' Mondo, and very few gentlemen," yet, the ascent would be perfectly easy, if one only knew the way, or could possibly find any native who did.

Sunday, Feb. 2, was the festival of Sta. Devota, and we heard the guns at Monaco firing incessantly like distan thunder. A great procession and an immense crowd o people celebrated the festa, but when we went the nex day, the humble little shrine was again quite deserted, except by two peasants, praying before its grated windows, under the tall cypresses.

MONTI AND THE GOOURG DI L'ORA.

Feb. 11.

THE Turin and Sospello road, which is still unfinished, and which passes the perfume manufactory of the princes of Monaco, now allows of a drive as far as Monti, about three miles from Mentone, a village, whose new church, embosomed in mountains, is visible long before you reach it.

The old road to Monti, which followed the eastern bank of the torrent, was called "La via della Pietra Scritta," on account of a very ancient stone slab, fixed against the rock, and engraved with a mysterious inscription in large characters. This has now been removed, and its present situation cannot be discovered. On the left side of the new road, as you ascend the valley, is a hole in the rock, where, in the memory of Theresine Paturine, the old donkey-driver, lived a little old woman, who was deemed a witch, and who was an object of great terror to the Mentonese children. When they were naughty, they were told that "La Catarina" would come and carry them off to her hole; and if any fell sick, she was supposed to have cast an evil eye upon them. But Catarina was really a good old woman, who spent much of her time in devout prayer in the churches, and who was entirely dependant on alms for her sustenance.

The church of Monti is a gingerbread gothic building, totally unlike everything else in the neighbourhood, and consequently it is much admired by the natives, though utterly unsuited to the scenery. A rope, fixed to the bell in the church tower, stretches across the road, and into the window of a house on the other side of it. This is the priest's window, and being of an apathetic disposition, the priest has the rope tied to him when he is in bed, that he may not be obliged to get up in order to ring the bell. In most of these remote villages, the priest is also the sacristan, sometimes he is likewise the schoolmaster, and he always tills his own ground. Wild mountain lavender grows in all the clefts of the rocks around Monti, and has leaves quite as sweet as the flowers of our lavender in England.

A short distance beyond this village a chasm in the rugged mountains on the right of the valley discloses a torrent rushing furiously down to join the broader stream below. This is the ravine of the Goourg di L'Ora, and to ascend into it, one may easily cross the stream by stepping stones, or in a rainy season, as in our case, by a bridge, which may usually be extemporized from the wood lying about and jerked across the stream. Hence one must scramble up the steep bank among the myrtles and cistus, to a path in the narrow depth of the gorge, where, behind a chaos of huge stones, the stream glides over the edge of the mountains in a long feathery fall, and shivers down into a little emerald green basin of still water.

Local legend long declared this tiny pool to be unfathomable, and the belief would still have existed, but that two years ago an English gentleman, who thought he was rendering a great service to science, had a line made many hundreds of palms long, to test its depth. But after spending several days up to his waist in water, trying to clear away some of the stones, which prevented his giving his line full play, he made the mournful discovery that he had been working all the time at the actual bottom of the hollow, which proved to be only six palms deep. Still it is a curious spot, and the view is fine over the desolate brown hills to the dreary looking town of Castiglione.

Above the cascade rises a mountain, which is pierced on one side of its summit by a natural tunnel, through which daylight appears. Near this, is the so-called "Grotta del Eremito," which has been the source of much interest and speculation. The difficulty and danger of approaching it, had prevented ts being visited for many years; but the report among the peasantry, that it had once been the abode of a hermit-saint, who had left curious memorials behind him, stimulated some of the English visitors into climbing its rock a short time ago, and successfully forcing an entrance. The recluse who lived there, must certainly have succeeded in avoiding intercourse with all human kind, for apart from the great difficulty of ascending to the cell, it is situated in such a wild retreat, that before the new road to Sospello was made, it could scarcely have been discovered from any of the neighbouring heights. The front is whitewashed, with a door, a window, and an inscription in red letters, as follows :—

Ñ R O S . A . . . . . O . .

L A   B A L M A   T E R . . .

L I . . H S P .   . II . .

L A N . . . .

1598

Of this, all that savants have been able to discover, is that in the old patois of Castiglione, "Balma" means cell or grotto, and that L. A. N. probably means "L'Anno." The cell is of irregular size, about twenty feet high, and thirty feet deep; it contains some shelves cut in the solid rock, and the words—

"CHRISTO LO FECE,
BERNARDO L'ABITO."

The return from the Goourg di L'Ora should be made by Castellare, which is reached by a wild walk fringed with blue hypaticas in spring. This first runs along a terrace, overlooking the mountain ranges, and then descends into a glen where there is a very picturesque old mill and gateway. We lingered so long here, that we only reached Castellare as darkness set in, and did not arrive at the cemetery of Mentone till two-hours-and-a-half later, after perils of darkness, on rocks, in torrent-beds, and over pathless olive terraces, which we cannot recommend others to encounter.

THE CARNIVAL AND LENT.

Feb. 14.

THE Carnival at Mentone is very different to those of Rome and Nice, but still is quite as much recognised in its own small way. The shops are full of hideous masks, with which even the poorest inhabitants contrive to adorn themselves towards evening, and the English inhabitants of Maison Gastaldy, and the other houses which border on the principal street, are obliged to keep their doors constantly locked, in order to prevent being interrupted, as it is quite in accordance with Mentonese etiquette, for anyone in a mask, to pay anyone else a visit if they can get in, and to stay as long as they like whether they are acquainted or not. The other day, an English lady answered the door-bell herself, when to her dismay she found four hideous masks with long bird's beaks at the door, who took advantage of her surprise to fly past her into the drawing room, where they startled the inmates by perching themselves on the armchairs and sofa, and by chattering together in shrill bird's language for some time. They turned out to be the dress-maker of the family and three young friends of hers. Another day the house butcher and his family paid a long visit in masks to the same people. François, the donkey man, rides through the streets in the evening on one of his own donkeys, dressed as an English lady, with another mask behind him as his man servant, carrying a camp stool and sketch-book. "But where does he get his dress from," I asked of a lady who had lived many years at Mentone. "Oh, there is no difficulty about that," she said, "any washerwoman would lend him one; we have learnt now to send as little as possible to the wash during the Carnival week, for when we send our things, they come back so worn and spoilt, that it is evident somebody has been dressed up in them every evening."

The Carnival ball at the Cirque had the unusual attraction to the English of being preceded by two Vaudevilles, in which the actors were all Mentonese ladies and gentlemen, who volunteered their services for the public amusement. The first Vaudeville was "Les petites affiches;" the second, "Les petites miseres de la vie humaine;" and nothing could have been more admirable than the acting, especially that of the Gastaldy family, whose dramatic talents are quite extraordinary. These performances had drawn such a crowd together, that the ball which took place afterwards was a great crush, and the heat most intense. According to an ancient Mentonese custom, all the maskers in the street had formerly the right of penetrating as far as the ball room, whenever they pleased during the Carnival, a privilege of which they availed themselves in large numbers. On these occasions the general dancing was stopped, and the masks being introduced, commenced a dance called the Montferrine, with those of the society, who they could engage as partners; after this dance the masks went away, but would return three or four times in the same evening. This custom, handed down from time immemorial, which united rich and poor, noble and bourgeois, has fallen into disuse only during the last few years. The first time an attempt was made to prevent the masks from entering, they tried to force their way in, asserting that no one had the right to abolish so ancient a custom, but the guard interfered, and they were obliged to submit. Since that time the balls at Mentone have been like those in any other provincial town.

Shrove Tuesday here had an imitation on a very small scale of the scenes which take place in the great Italian cities on that day. The Strada St. Michaele was crowded towards three o'clock with almost the whole population of the place, who stood in two thick lines against the houses, prepared to gape and shout at the absurd figures in masks and costume, who kept running backwards and forwards up the middle of the street. The dresses were filthy and shabby to the last degree, but very ridiculous. Sometimes an old lady in spectacles would pass riding on a donkey, and enveloped in a coloured hood, which, when she came near, disclosed the moustache and pointed black beard of a man. Sometimes an old general hobbled by in cocked hat and uniform, apparently very much the worse for warfare, and supported by his affectionate daughters; here was seen a party of gipsies, with copper-coloured faces, jabbering in qualch: there four ghosts deadly white and sewn up together in the same sheet, from which only their heads projected, while they stood upright in a cart, and uttered horrid shrieks at intervals. Then, amid all the rag-tag and bob-tail of the place, six young men of the best Mentonese families, who had first dined in costume at the Hotel de Londres, spent the afternoon in chasing each other on donkeys, which were trained to perform a dance for the occasion in the middle of the street. At four o'clock the tumult began to subside, but several masks were loitering about till quite late in the evening, and a hideous creature dressed entirely in yellow pursued me all the way to a party, like the yellow mask at Pisa, in Wilkie Collins' story. At night there was the ball for the lower classes, to which our donna went, and danced till five in the morning, for, as she said, it was always "Encore une polka, encore une valse, pendant toute la nuit."

The bay was the scene of a curious adventure on Sunday, when a Genoese Marchese went out with two ladies in a pleasure-boat, which was upset a little beyond the fort, by a sudden gust of wind. The Marchese swam to shore, and the two ladies had presence of mind to float quietly upon their crenolines, till a boat put out from the fort and picked them up. Afterwards, their quaint life-preservers were hung out to dry from an upper window in the Pension Anglaise, where they were staying, and became quite an object of pilgrimage for the whole afternoon to the idle people of Mentone.

A grand pic-nic has been given at the Madone, by the English artists, living at Mentone, and their friends. It had been fixed for the preceding Monday, but was put off because it poured with rain, since, as the disappointed coachman from whom we had ordered our carriage announced, "le bon Dieu oubliait que c'etait le jour de fête." However, at last, both day and pic-nic were charming, if pic-nic it could be called, when it was more like a very smart London breakfast, given in the old refectory of the convent. Afterwards there was dancing beneath the pine trees in the garden, while the Mentonese ladies and gentlemen sat and watched indefatigably, an amusement which they preferred to playing at games, for as it was Lent, they were not able to join in the dancing. The French visitors, however, *were* able to dance, for the Pope had given them dispensation for the Carême, because, as they said, "Cà nous gene trôp." From time immemorial it was the rule at Mentone, for all the young inhabitants to dance after vespers under these pines of the Madone, and it has been only quite of late years that this custom has fallen into disuse. A Duke of York, (no one quite knows what Duke of York) lived in the adjoining Pavillion, in the time of the early princes, before the first French revolution. It is said he set up the column on the Cape St. Martin, of which the remains are still standing.

This place looks more rich and fertile than ever. New flowers come out every day, and the gardens are really splendid. Camelias bloom luxuriantly in the open air. The Gorbio valley is full of anemones, which carpet the ground under the oranges; there are several varieties, the single purple anemone, the bright single scarlet and the double scarlet, which is green when it first comes out, and which we have in our gardens in England, and also the star-like single anemone, whose colour varies from the palest lilac to pink. Everywhere the air is scented by the orange and lemon blossoms, which are as valuable as the fruit itself, from the price they fetch in the perfume manufactories. The oranges are much hardier than the lemons, and in dry weather will bear seven degrees of frost, while the lemons perish at four or five degrees; but if a frost sets in after rainy weather, a much slighter degree of cold is fatal to both.

Old Theresine told me one day that the fertility of Mentone was all owing to Eve.

"To Eve," I said, "why what did she do?"

"Oh, she gave us the gift of Paradise."

"The gift of Paradise, and what is that?"

"Oh, don't you know," she said, "that though Adam and Eve were very much hurried when they were turned

THE CARNIVAL AND LENT. 149

out of Paradise, and had not time to consider what they should take with them, close by the gate of Paradise there grew a lemon tree, and Eve, as she passed by, had just time to snatch one single fruit, which she hid in her apron as she went out. Afterwards, when she was wandering about on the earth, she threw the lemon down upon Mentone, where it grew and multiplied, and so it is that we have here the one thing which really came out of Paradise." Afterwards we found old Theresine's story in the following ballad :—

"Just within Eden's gate
  A lovely tree had root;
The leaves were of the richest green,
  Of pale gold hue the fruit.

It chanced upon that mournful day,
  When thro' the portals past,
Our parents twain, Eve turned again
  That she might look her last.

O'erwhelmed with grief her bowers to leave,
  Just as she hurried through,
In haste she stretched her hand and snatched
  A lemon from the bough.

'I'll treasure this,' she said, 'until
  On the bleak earth I find,
One spot so fair, as to reflect,
  The joys I've left behind.'

Upon a mountain high she stood,
  And sadly she looked down,
As the dull earth beneath her lay,
  With briars and thorns o'ergrown.

Till in the far far west she spied
  A bay whose sunny coast,
Fringing the sapphire wave, recall'd
  The Eden she had lost.

She flung her treasure there, and cried,
   'Shed forth thy seeds to grow,
And make of this one smiling spot,
   A Paradise below.'

The lemon grew and multiplied,
   From that day unto this,
And at Mentone, mortals find
   A taste of Eden's bliss."

Another story, which is told by the Mentonese to prove the extraordinary fertility of the soil, is, that the large handsome tree shrub, which stands in front of the Maison d'Ardoin, near the Bazaar, and which forms the chief ornament of the Rue St. Michel, originated in the walking stick of a gentleman, which he stuck into the ground near the door, when he went to pay a visit to a lady who lived in the house. Coming out, he forgot it, and going back to recover it three days after, he found his stick sprouting and growing where he had left it, after which it attained to its present size.

CASTIGLIONE AND GHIANDOLA.

Feb. 24.

WE have had a second rainy season for the last three weeks, that is to say, we have not been able to calculate upon fine weather and to fix days for expeditions as we used to do, though after all, as Monsieur Trenca reminds us, it has been only "un jour de pluie, un jour de soleil; çà rècompense." Indeed the bad weather we have had seems to have been universally expected. A shopman told us the other day that "March is always a bad month, because that is the time when men did kill God." The consequence is, that according to the Mentonese proverb, "cora ra fouant ex secca se conosce or pres d r'aija," (When the fountain is dry, then one knows the value of water), we have begun to regret that we did not do more while the sun shone and the sky was cloudless.

However, on the 23rd, the artist visitors were induced to snatch at a rainless morning which took them by surprise, and we all set off for Castiglione at half-past eight, having annexed three donkeys to our party. Our path turned off to the left from the Monti road before it reached the hill, and ascended by a steep narrow cleft between banks now covered with violets and fly orchis, into an old pine wood, on the mountain ridge, which rises up between the Monti and Cabruare valleys, and through this wood it continued to wind for the greater part of the way. The myrtles here are quite magnificent, some of them as large as the largest laurestinus bushes in England, and there are four different varieties. Many other curious shrubs grow between the red stems of the pine trees; but chiefly cistuses, heaths, and capparis spinosa—the flowering caper plant. The view towards St. Agnese is magnificent, the town and the campanile of the church appearing on the other side of its castellated rock, which descends in immense precipices to the plain.

We had just gone through every degree of rapturous exclamation over the views, the flowers, and the windings of the wood itself, when the path opened upon a scene which was the more startling from its contrast with what we had left. Behind, all was a radiant Eden; before us spread for miles a wilderness of bleak, arid, desolate precipices, without a tree, or a patch of verdure to cheer the eye, which wanders on to the bleak distant snows, over billow upon billow of stony aclivity, on which not a human habitation is to be seen, except where Castiglione rises grey and ghost-like from the mountain side. Even the town itself is as unlike a town as possible, no doors, no windows, no gates, apparently no inhabitants, and no visible approach to it up the precipitous rocks on which it is seated, so that we should scarcely have believed it to be a town at all, save for the pointed campanile of its church, which overtops the other buildings. Happily the morning was grey and cloudy, or we should have been completely scorched, whilst toiling on along the arid, barren, shadowless slopes of rock, which are exposed to the full beams of the burning sun throughout the summer, while all the winter long, the icy frost-laden wind beats furiously upon them and upon the unprotected town which looks over a Siberian desert of snow. My pleasure all along had been a good deal marred by the conduct of my donkey "La Bianca," who after making all possible contortions, kicking, and trying to run down the sides of every embankment we came to, finally succeeded in pitching me off on the road. However, soon after we reached the stone which marks the entrance into the Sardinian territory, it was no longer a question whether it was worth while any more to struggle with the unruly steed, for the road which had gradually become narrower, (though till lately the only road from Mentone to Sospello and Turin), now ceased altogether, having been carried away far down the mountain in an éboulement, and the people of Castiglione, if any able bodied inhabitants exist there, having been much too lazy to repair it. So here we left our donkeys and took all our possessions with us, as we had not much expectation of ever seeing the animals again, for of our two intelligent companions Constantine and Theresine (la jeune), the former could never understand us in the least, whether we spoke in French, Italian or Patois, and the latter only understood us to act exactly contrary to all we desired. When we reached the foot of the Castiglione rock, tiny windows began to show themselves on the outside of the town, made almost like loopholes for the better fortification of the place, while all the larger windows look inwards to the street. Some of these are mediæval gothic, with a central pillar and sculptured capital dividing them. At length a rock-hewn staircase revealed itself, which winding round the steep, brought us to the narrow gateway of the town, where, when you stand upon the rocky platform in front, you discover a little world of mountain vallies beneath, each with a torrent curling and twisting through its windings.

Most quaint of all the quaint towns in this wonderful neighbourhood is Castiglione; its steep streets twist so much that you never see more than three doors before you; the approaches to its houses are mere footings cut in the bare rocks; and its quaint storm-beaten campanile rises among yellow and orange-coloured houses, each with a painted image, or ornamented roof-coping. And then the inhabitants, who make one think that all the old women in the whole Riviera must have been collected and sent into exile here, such multitudes of old crones do you see, while not another living creature is visible, except the cocks and hens which make the street look like one great poultry yard, and which seem to be the sole nutriment of the crones, for what else, animal, vegetable, or mineral is there for them to eat.

At Mentone, the morning had been hot and sultry, and when we got home people were complaining of the heat, but here as we sat down before the south gate to draw, the wind was shrill and piercing, our fingers were so benumbed that we could hardly hold our pencils, and we were truly glad when at three o'clock the donkeys arrived in safety, and we were able to attend to the warning of the rain clouds that it was time for departure. We returned by the new road to Sospello, which winds above the hills beyond Monti, and which is now near completion. Long before we reached Monti the rain began to fall, so we hurried home and arrived at Mentone at half-past six, wet and tired, but quite sure that we should be delighted again to go through the same fatigue, in order to spend another day at weird out of the world Castiglione.

For those who wish to extend their expedition beyond Castiglione, a quick descent of a little more than six hours leads from the tunnel near the town to Sospello, (four hours' walk from Mentone), where there is a clean though simple inn, at which a tolerable meal may be obtained. Sospello is a long straggling town on the banks of a river, with an ancient, but modernized cathedral, and many quaint houses resting on open arcades of very early Italian architecture. The town possesses two bridges, one of which is very picturesque. A carriage may be obtained here to go to Ghiandola, which is a beautiful drive of about three or four hours. The lower parts of these valleys are devoted to pasturage, olives and mulberry trees; the higher sides of the hills are grass-grown, and run up into woods of stone pine, above which they become arid and bare. The descent upon Ghiandola from a "Col." which is crossed midway, is very beautiful. Olives abound as you approach the town, around which are scattered several handsome villas belonging to wealthy Piedmontese families.

It takes about three hours to walk from Sospello to Ghiandola, where there is a charming mountain inn, (Hotel des Etrangers); the hostess, a widow, being very attentive and a capital cook. The inn itself is situated at the bottom of a valley, but, by ascending in any direction, the most beautiful views are immediately obtained. For the artist, the botanist, and the geologist, Ghiandola would afford endless amusement, and should be visited in the spring for the sake of its green woods and mountain breezes.

Breglio, only one mile from Ghiandola, affords magnificent subjects for sketching. There the Roya, a rocky-bedded mountain torrent, rushes beneath a bridge, which is very lofty and wide in its span, and whose piers rest upon rocks projecting boldly into the stream. Here the road takes a turn, where a remarkable chapel stands on the edge of the rock. Beyond the bridge, the torrent is seen rushing from the town, which has a wonderful collection of campaniles, turrets, and a square tower, with mountains rising beyond.

An interesting excursion may be made in seven hours from Ghiandola to Ventimiglia; two mule paths leading thither down the valley of the Roya, on its right bank. For this purpose mules may be obtained at Ghiandola. Another point for an excursion is Saorgio, about two hours' walk from Ghiandola, a town curiously perched on a rock, and approached by a road winding in continuous zig-zags. By the carriage road Saorgio is five or six miles distant. The scenery of the mule path from Saorgio to Dolceacqua is said to be very fine.

ON DONKEYS TO PEGLIA.

March 4.

THIS expedition, which so many talk of and so few carry out, we have accomplished at last.

Saturday, March 2, was a beautiful morning, and the sun, which rose in crimson splendour from the sea, had soon dried up the thick dew which lay upon the ground, and was scorching the barren sides of the hills.

We assembled our party at 7 a.m. before Maison Gastaldy, and soon were on our donkeys, clambering up the steep path in the pine woods to St. Agnese, through the delicious luxuriant undergrowth of myrtle, arbutus, rosemary, and Mediterranean heath, now in full bloom. The ground too on the more open banks was blue with hepaticas and violets, and here and there a tuft of English-looking primroses was peeping forth. The road had been a good deal injured in places by the heavy rain, but still we contrived to find a passage, and reached the ridge of the mountains below St. Agnese before ten o'clock; then, instead of ascending to the village, we halted at a desolate little chapel on the edge of the precipice, where we gave our donkeys a breakfast of rosemary in the porch, and held a council-general.

This is considered the extreme limit of donkey's powers,

and it was hard work to persuade Theresine to go any further, though the temptation of an additional five francs for each donkey, proved irresistible in the end, in spite of her declaring we meant to take her, "jusqu' à la maison même du diable."

Beyond St. Agnese, the path to Peglia turns to the left, and crossing a ridge of hill continues to wind constantly in the same direction, till it reaches its destination. The scenery is wild and desolate in the extreme, the arid hills covered with loose stones, but with scarcely a vestige of vegetation to vary their dead brown, which melts into deep purple in more distant ranges, while above and beyond, snowy Alps rise ghost-like against the sky. We did not meet a creature between the two villages, except a solitary cow-herd, watching some calves who were trying to extract a miserable subsistence from the few tufts of short grass which grew between the rocks. All was bleak, gloomy desolation, till after about two hours' walk, on turning a corner, a magnificent view revealed itself. In the distance was the blue, mirror-calm sea, with the further islands of Hyeres, and the nearer of Cannes. Beyond the jagged range of purple Estrelles, other capes and promontories, unseen from below, extended their pale forms across the distance; beneath our feet, the mountains were broken into a hundred deep chasms and purple ravines, while the path to Peglia wound serpentlike at the foot of gigantic precipices. A short distance beyond this, on turning a corner, by a ruined chapel, Peglia itself is first seen in its solitary valley. The church bells were ringing as we descended, otherwise the town bursting upon us suddenly in that desolate spot, would have seemed uncannily still and dreamlike, with the rugged precipices closing it in on either side, and the grim grey church standing like a sentinel before the groups of brown houses sleeping in the purple haze, and backed by the sunlit sea, while patches of brilliant green grass here alone varied the monotony of the brown hill sides.

The first view was so striking, that some of the party staid to sketch, and when they rejoined the others, they found them comfortably seated on the little platform in front of the church, overlooking the town and valley, where the hospitality of the curé had already set out a table with a bottle of excellent wine, bread, cheese and fruit, of which he pressed all to partake. Afterwards he exhibited his church, which is exceedingly interesting both within and without.

The floor is still formed by the living rock, and many of the pillars are masses of rock, which have never been moved from their original situation, and are merely cut into huge square blocks. The gigantic font formed from a single block of porphyry, and the granite basins for holy water, of rude and primitive shape, are very curious. A chapel with a painted ceiling, has some strange old pictures of the life of Christ, and some of the modern pictures are grotesque, especially one of a party of saints dragging an ugly little naked devil in chains. A queer-looking wooden arm stretches out a crucifix from the side of the pulpit, certainly a most restful invention for the preacher, if it was necessary for some one to hold it so. Altogether any artist who loves picturesque interiors, might make some capital drawings inside the church at Peglia, and though the building is not of the "premier siècle," as the old curé declared, it is equally interesting to the architect. Both alike will be aghast to hear that it will soon be seen no more, and that the people of Peglia, who think five minutes' walk too far to go to church, are going to pull it down, in order to build a church nearer home with the materials. Could not the Architectural Society of France be induced to interfere?

The rarity of visits from strangers at Peglia, seemed greatly to enhance their value. We were accompanied over the town, not only by the curé, but by the mayor, who, his companion informed us, was the only person in the place who knew any thing. Both were equally amazed at the interest their antiquities inspired, and at our rushing to examine and copy inscriptions, which they had passed a hundred times without ever noticing. The chief extent of the knowledge of each seemed to be that Peglia was the oldest place in the department, and that you have only to look around you to prove it. The streets are narrow and dark, and the doorways are arched and gloomy, the windows are frequently gothic, with a central pillar and richly carved capital. Through a dark vaulted passage, you ascend to what was once an old palace of the Lascaris, now containing a school and the Hotel de Ville, which is a common-place room with an Armoire, filled with what the mayor called "the Gothic Manuscripts," really Latin MSS. on vellum in gothic characters, which we had not time to decipher. From the rocks above this, the view looking down over the brown roofs of the town, with its broken fragments of encircling walls, its gothic remains, and a modern dome, is very striking and peculiar.

"Could we not stay till to-morrow, and could he not give us all beds, with the assistance of Monsieur le Maire, and could he not send an express to Mentone to prevent our friends being alarmed," said the hospitable curé. And "was not to-morrow their civil festa, when little imitation cannons would fire all day long in the most diverting manner," echoed the mayor; "and was it not utterly impossible for us to return to Mentone that night," chorused both. But, unfortunately, "to-morrow" was Sunday, and as we did not feel we could stay away two whole days, we were obliged to set off on our return at four o'clock, in spite of the wrathful expostulations of Theresine, who was certain that we meant to kill both her and her donkeys, and who had already looked out lodgings for the repose of each in the hope of assisting at the festa in the morning.

Peglia looked lovely against the green sunset sky, as our procession wound up the hills on our return. The curé went with us to set us on our way, and returned after the first two miles, with a donation for his poor, with which he was highly delighted, and a commission to find out all he possibly could about the antiquities and traditions of his native place.

We took another way home, which is much shorter, but very steep, the path for some distance being quite lost in the bed of a torrent, after which it crosses the lower slopes of Mont Garillon, whence it descends upon Gorbio by a ridge, from whence the town is seen, quaintly cresting its round-topped hill. We did not reach Gorbio till nightfall, and the rest of the way was in almost pitch darkness, so that we had to hold each other's hands to prevent being lost. In this state we sank up to our knees in the deep mud which the rains had left, and a lady, who chose to walk alone, fell over one of the high olive terraces, but contrived to scramble up again without being hurt.

Between eight and nine we regained Mentone.

EXCURSION TO NICE AND PEGLIONE.

March 18.

ABOUT three miles on this side of Nice is the little village of Potervium, a place which no one can mistake, if they look out for an imitation soldier with flowing hair, who is represented jovially drinking wine under the wall of a little public-house. Here a path strikes off to the right and then taking a turn to the left, through some olive gardens, leads to the top of the hill which forms the background of lovely Villafranca, which looks strangely eastern as it stands on the edge of the sea, backed by stony declivities, its brown roofs interspersed with domes of churches and convents, while here and there a dark mass of cypress rises against the blue water. In the narrow streets, heaps of oranges, dates, figs, and plums, are piled up for sale on either side of the broad sunny pavement. Below is the quay, where the deep blue sea washes up among yellow rocks under the gaily-painted houses, while a number of boats ply to and fro to carry visitors to the large men-of-war which lie at anchor in the harbour.

The town was built from 1295 to 1303, by Charles of Anjou, king of Sicily and count of Provence, and owes its name to the privileges which it obtained from its foundation. Its climate is said to be one of the mildest and most

equable on the whole Riviera. A charming excursion may be made from hence to the Presqu'ile of St. Hospice, on whose eastern point is a ruined fort, built by Victor Amadeus I, and destroyed in 1706 by Marshal Berwick. Near this is the ruined chapel of St. Hospice, a pious anchorite of the sixth century, who prophesied the victories of the Lombards, ("Venient in Galliam Longobardi et vastabunt civitates septem"). In the Presqu'ile was situated the famous Moorish fortress of Fraxinet, which gave the Saracens their great hold upon this coast.

A lovely road through the olive woods and fields, starred with pink anemones, leads from Villafranca to Nice, where we found the Hotel Paradis both comfortable and reasonable. The number of people, and the noise and bustle of the place, seemed quite astonishing after so many months of quiet Mentone, while the town itself reminded us of Paris, by its fine quays along the river Paillon, its boulevards and handsome stone houses; but certainly at Paris, there is no view of distant mountains, across ever-varying waves of sapphire sea, and no tall palm tree, to be streaked with gold by the rays of the setting sun. Here is realized the description given by Delille in his Jardins :—

> "Oh Nice, heureux séjour, montagnes renommeés,
> De lavende, de thyme, de citron parfumées,
> Que de fois sous tes plants d'oliviers toujours verts,
> Dont la pâleur s'unit au sombre, azur des mers,
> J'égarai mes regards sur ce théâtre immense."

The town contains about 30,000 inhabitants. The shops are good but excessively dear. The native manufacture of carved olive wood especially, is five times as expensive as work of the same kind at Sorrento. Pensions at Nice are reasonable, costing about eight francs a day. The best are the Pension Rivoir, 21, Chemin des Anglais; the Pension d'Italie, Rue de France; and the Pension Visconti, in a delightful situation on the Cimies, the cost of which, including everything, is ten francs a-day. The hire of a donkey is three francs for the whole day.

There are few antiquities in Nice. The castle, which looks down upon the eastern extremity of the town, was blown up by the Duke of Berwick in 1706. The "Croix de Marbre," standing under a picturesque little canopy, opposite to the English church, commemorates the so-called conference in 1538, between Pope Paul III., Charles V., and Francis I. Massena was born, the son of a small woollen-draper, in a narrow street near Sta. Reparata; Garibaldi was born in a house near the Boulevard de l'Imperatrice, where his brother was murdered. The Nizzard dialect is interesting, as being almost the same as the ancient Romane language in which the Troubadours wrote and sung. The inhabitants of Nice are not rich, the incomes of the richest not exceeding one thousand or twelve hundred pounds a-year.

The day after our arrival at Nice, we started early to ascend the hills which form the western background of the town. The roads are quite different to those of Mentone, no longer narrow mountain paths, or often mere staircases cut in the arid rock, but broad cart tracks winding through avenues of olives into fields on the high grounds, which are now carpeted by bright green flax or young corn; while beyond, the glorious snowy ranges are revealed in their full extent, resting upon the nearer purple hills. On a high point is the Pin de Bellet, marking the summit of a hill, covered with the vineyards producing the famous wine of that name, which is of great excellence, though the fact, that at least a thousand times as much is sold every year as the vineyard could possibly produce, shows how much it is adulterated. In a hollow, buried amongst the olives, is the hamlet of St. Romain. Its lovely painted campanile, with its old houses and the Doric portico of the church, broken by the olive trees, whose delicate branches cast flickering shadows across its pillars, is one of the most picturesque objects in the district. Beyond is a natural terrace, which looks down upon the great bed of the Var, closed in by snowy mountains, while along its opposite bank lie the "Seven Villages," each full of characteristic beauty. The highest of these, nestling under strange perpendicular rocks, is St. Jannet, whose women have all the reputation of being witches; while above on the mountain is a huge old nut-tree, where the witches are believed to hold their Sabbat. We came down from the mountains upon Les Scires, where a carriage was waiting for us, and whence we had a lovely drive home by the sheltered lanes of St. Augustin, bordered with narcissus and anemones.

The next day we set off at ten in a carriage to Levens, by a road which passes first along the left bank of the Paillon, and afterwards follows the course of a smaller stream. On the left, on an olive-clad hill rises the Franciscan Convent of Cimies. Beyond and below, is the finer Benedictine Convent of St. Pons, founded in 775 by St. Siagre, who is said to have been a son of Carloman and nephew of Charlemagne the Great. The original building was destroyed by the Saracens in 890, but the convent was rebuilt in 999 by Fredonius, bishop of Nice. During the revolution it was suppressed and turned into a military hospital, but was restored again in 1835 by Monseigneur Galvano, as a convent of lay-monks. Before its gates grew a large elm tree, (cut down in 1760) beneath which the inhabitants of Nice assembled in 1388, to place themselves under the rule of Amadeus VII., Duke of Savoy, surnamed the Red. The act of this donation was dated, "Sub ulmo Sancti Pontii et ante monasterium." In 1835, bishop Galvano marked the site of the elm by a marble slab, bearing an inscription which still commemorates the event. Beyond the convent, and near the remains of an ancient temple, is a tiny chapel which overhangs the road on a precipitous rock. Here it is said St. Pons was beheaded, a saint who is reported to have been a Roman senator, who embraced Christianity in the time of the Emperor Philip, whom he converted to his own faith; but, in the persecution which followed, he was obliged to fly from Rome and take refuge at Cimies, where he was arrested, and put to death, by order of the Emperor Claudius. According to Cardinal Baronius, this happened on May 11th, 261. The head of St. Pons is declared by the natives to have jumped from the top of the rock into the Paillon, whence two lighted torches arose out of the water to meet it; between these it sailed in triumph down the river to the Mediterranean, and thence to Marseilles, where it landed on a rock, upon which another chapel was built to its honour.

A short distance hence the Chateau St. André, still inhabited by the count of that name, almost blocks up the valley, crowning a hill whose sides are picturesquely clothed with old ilex trees. Beyond is the Grotto St. André, where the torrent passes under the road, through a natural tunnel in the tufa rock. Here the highway enters a fine gorge, which is like some of the passages in the Val Moutiers, the perpendicular rocks fringed with pines, standing out against the sky, while the torrent struggles and tosses below. A ruined wall on the rock, which looks like a hermitage, marks the spot where the French, during their occupation of Nice, successfully defended this gorge against the Piedmontese, who tried to make a descent through it upon the town. Beyond this point the road to Levens is uninteresting. On the left is the turn which leads to the Grotto of Falicon, called by the natives the "Grotta di Ratapignata," on account of the number of bats which inhabit it. Beyond this, Mont Chauve is seen above the lower hills. On the right, cresting a hill, are conspicuous the ruined walls of the large village of Chateauneuf, now entirely deserted and abandoned to ghosts and owls, but striking, and well worthy of a visit.

Levens itself is an ugly village on a barren hill; its streets were crowded with filthy children, all ill with the hooping cough, of which they gave us the full benefit while we were drawing. At its summit is a large church, with an inscription recording the feelings of the people "devoto e recognoscente," for the very small favour of two Piedmontese princes having once passed through their town. On our return we stopped to see Tourette, a village, with a highly painted church, surrounded by mountains, and an old castle now turned into a dwelling house, with a curious reef of pointed rocks, stretching from it down the valley.

The following afternoon I had a delightful walk through the shady olive groves, which overhang the Paillon to Cimies, the Civitas Cimeliensis of the Romans, but more remarkable now for its convent and lovely views, than for the obscure but vaunted remains of a Nymphæum, and a temple believed to be that of Diana, in the garden of Count Garin, or the ruins of an amphitheatre which still preserves its oval form and ancient steps, and which is called by the natives, "Il tino delle fade," or "the fairy's bath." From the garden of the Maison Garin a subterranean passage is said to extend under the Paillon to the little chapel of St. Roch, near Mont Vinaigrier. In this passage the natives say that the devil sits at a table, with a golden horn upon it, whilst a golden goat and a golden kid stand by his side; for one half-hour in the day the devil sleeps, and if, during that half-hour, any one had the courage to go down, they might carry off the golden goat and the golden kid in safety, and would be enriched for life. Local gossip asserts that this feat was nearly accomplished thirty years ago, when some men went down, and seeing the devil sitting asleep, caught up the golden kid and ran as hard as they could; but they had come too late in the half-hour, for before they reached the end of the passage, the devil awoke and pursued them; they dropped the golden kid and fled for their lives, but before they could escape, the devil had touched them, and they all died dreadful deaths a few weeks afterwards. The garden is said to be haunted, and mysterious voices have been heard in it by those who pass on the road at night, which are accounted for by supernatural agency; but they may be explained by the existence of an extraordinary echo, through which a person walking on the upper road to Cimies, when he arrives at this villa, may distinctly hear every word spoken by a person walking on the lower road which leads to the same place.

The Franciscan convent of Cimies stands in a piazza, which is filled with fine old cork trees, beneath whose shadow stands a curious cross, on which the Crucified One is represented with wings, as a cherubim. The interior of the church is handsomely painted in fresco, and contains a good specimen of the work of Ludovico Brea, born in 1651, the best artist ever produced by Nice. Cimies possesses a milder climate than Nice, and has some good lodging-houses and pensions, which are much resorted to by those who prefer a quiet country residence to the gaiety and the dust of the town. Below, about half-a-mile from Nice, is the picturesque convent of St. Barthelemy, with an altar piece said to have been brought from Rhodes.

The next morning we had a specimen of what Nice dust could be; in a minute after leaving the door, one was covered from head to foot, as if dipped in a flour tub, one's hair was steeped in the thick white powder, and one's lips were plastered with dust. To see the way was impossible; the whole air was a thick mass of prickly white particles; one could only trust to the wall for guidance. Under these circumstances we were certainly glad to drive away in a sweeping white tornado to Drap, on the way to Peglione.

We left the Turin road close to a stone bridge over the Paillon, and thence began to ascend towards the mountains by a winding mule path. This road was formerly infested by a notorious gang of bandits, and near this is the Fontaine de Giallier, where, in the time of the first empire, the carriage of the Marchioness of Bute, travelling to Turin, was stopped by a number of these men, who carried off all her valuables and diamonds. For a long time before this attempts had been made in vain to capture the brigands, but that day the gendarmes were more successful. Lady Bute had with her some opium which she was accustomed to take in order to assist her in sleeping by the way; the robbers thought that they had discovered a bottle of liqueur, and some of them drank of it. In a little while they grew drowsy and lay down among the corn near the wayside to rest a little; there sleep overcame them, and there they were found some hours after, by the gendarmes who were in search of them.

Almost all the band were discovered, and it was learnt with astonishment, that many men belonging to the noble families of Nice had formed a part of it and lived upon their plunder, even inviting the authorities of the town to dinner, who never had the least suspicion of the connexion of their hosts with the famous bandits. The robbers had the wit to take care that their dinners were always given the day after some remarkable robbery, the further to evade suspicion, and had it not been for Lady Bute's laudanum, they would probably never have been found out. Three of them were condemned to death. Many of Lady Bute's diamonds were never discovered. One of the band alone, a man named Belloni, escaped to France. Many years after, his son and daughter-in-law returned to Nice in good circumstances, and the lady appeared at a ball wearing a magnificent diamond ornament. "Ah, c'est des diamants de Gaillier," was the universal remark.

It is curious that a grandson of this same Belloni, living at the picturesque old Ray Mill, near Nice, as a miller, rendered that place also notorious by an atrocious crime. He was celebrated as a marksman. One day when some French soldiers were passing by, one of them stooped down to wash the hem of his trowsers in the brook. The miller had been boasting of his skill to his friends; "I will shoot that man through the heart for forty sous," said he to his neighbour. The friend said "Done," thinking it was a joke, and the miller instantly shot the man through the heart.

But to return to Peglione, which soon appears most strikingly situated on the top of a conical rock, rising high above the forests of olives, against the wild extraordinary peaks of the surrounding mountains. The town itself is exceedingly picturesque, and has a broad terrazone, with old tumble-down houses on one side, and a little chapel painted with quaint frescoes on the other. The view of Peglione from the side towards Peglia (one hour distant), is the most striking scene in all this neighbourhood. The village itself occupies the foreground, on the top of a gigantic precipice, around the foot of which winds the river, while beyond billow upon billow of purple hills fall back to join the distant snow mountains. The road hence to Turbia is wild, desolate, and rugged, and we were heartily glad when we reached the village and found a carriage from Mentone awaiting us, with bread, oranges, and a bottle of Vino d'Asti, which had been left for us to atone for the absence of our friends who had promised to meet us at Peglione. They had been obliged to return to Peglia after the ascent of Mont Agel, by one of the ladies, who had been represented as a first rate walker, falling flat down on her back upon the rocks, and declaring that she could not possibly go a step further.

PASSION WEEK AND EASTER.

Good Friday, March 29.

LENT has hung heavily upon the Mentonese, who are obliged by their priests to keep it very strictly, and all look forward eagerly to an emancipation, which will allow their mouths to eat bonbons, and their legs to dance cotillons once more. Even the poor donkey-women, when out with us on a long day's expedition, have been obliged to refuse the poor remains of our luncheon, and to look on with wistful eyes and hungry stomachs, while dogs fed on the sandwiches that were left.

Palm Sunday was a hot sultry day, and when I went up the steps of St. Michele, an hour before the service at our own church, I found not only the interior of the building, but the piazza outside, filled with a steaming, heaving crowd. All were pressing eagerly but slowly towards the high altar, where the curé was giving his benediction to the long white waving palm branches, which each carried in his hand; some of the palms being left in their natural state, some twisted and curled in curious devices, with the leaves plaited half-way up into the shape of crosses and circles, and then rising into a feathery plume. Many of these, which were made by a bedridden man, were really beautiful. Some were laden with bread, figs, olives, oranges, &c., all the fruits of the earth, that they also might receive a blessing, while those of the children were covered with sugarplums and playthings. When all the palm-bearing people had filed up to the altar on one side of the church, and, having received their benediction, had regained the street by the other, the actual solemnities of the day commenced, and the clergy, bearing long palm-branches in their hands and chaunting as they came, slowly advanced down the centre of the church to the great western door, which was closed. There they remained singing the 24th Psalm. Meanwhile the chaunt was echoed in subdued strains from the piazza outside, till on reaching a particular point ("Lift up your heads ye everlasting doors, and the king of glory shall come in?") the great doors were thrown open, and a second procession entered, bearing the Host and followed by a great multitude of people. Then the first procession waving their long palm-branches and chaunting, preceded them to the altar, where the usual morning service was continued. After Vespers, a service here almost exclusively attended by women, a celebrated Dominican friar preached. We went again at sunset to be present at the Salut or Benediction. At this time the church was perfectly thronged by people of both sexes, among whom the most absolute silence prevailed, not a limb or a lip moving, when after the blessing a short interval was left for silent prayer.

On Holy Thursday and for two days afterwards the church clock which sets the time for the whole of Mentone is stopped, and does not strike again till "Christ is risen." The hours are told by people rattling bones in a box, which they call "rattling Judas' bones." This however is not only done at the stated hours, for a whole procession of children disturbed us very early in the morning, by coming to rattle their boxes at the chapel of St. Anne, under our windows, and at 6 p.m., half the population assembled on principle during three days, to "grind Judas' bones" together for a considerable time in the principal church. Yesterday evening, at eight o'clock, we set out to see the ceremonies, and found the town illuminated, lines of little lamps gleaming along the top of Il Portico, and flickering in every window. We went first to the church of St. John Baptist, where the Penitents Noirs in their black robes were waiting to hear a sermon, but the crowd and the heat were so great that we fled to the church of Il Conceptione, where we found the Penitents Blancs, with whom the chief business of the evening rests, assembled in white dresses, with ghastly sort of white night-caps on their heads, around a statue, which the people call "Jesu lié," and which is held by them in the utmost veneration. The statue, which represents the Saviour bound to a column, while an angel is performing an extraordinary gymnastic over his head, was lit up to-night by an immense number of wax candles, which flickered painfully upon the contorted limbs and agonized countenance. A jesuit was preaching, but though his action was most violent, and though every now and then he dashed off his cap and threw his hands into the air, with an outcry which made the church re-echo, the poorer people seemed too much taken up with the image to attend to him. When the sermon was over, twelve pilgrims were made to sit down in a circle in the middle of the church, and their feet were washed by the penitents, who kissed first the feet and then the face of each, as he finished the operation. We were amused to recognize one of the penitents, who grinned in passing us, as our comical old postman. Soon we went out into the cool starlit piazza, where, sitting on the terrace, between the churches, we had a very pretty view of the two processions, the white penitents as they emerged from the Conceptione, bearing their old-fashioned silvered lanthorns on poles, their great black crucifix, and the famous statue; and the black penitents, as they wound up the hill to St. Michaele.

On entering this church, which was entirely hung with black, and only lighted by the candles on the altar and the great chandelier in the centre, we found one of the aisles closed by a huge transparency of the crucifixion, on which the gaze of the whole multitude was directed, while they continued to chaunt the penitential psalms together in the most congregational way. We sat in one of the side chapels, and there watched the two processions enter and make the circuit of the church. The whole service was chaunted, and the singing was very universal and devotional.

This morning at four o'clock, "the Pilgrim Preacher of the Riviera" addressed the people in St. Michaele. He preaches at this early hour in order to secure the attendance of the work people, who are unavoidably obliged to go out on Good Friday to labour in the mountain olive groves. The congregations at this time are always numerous, and his sermons are said to be most striking, and so touching, that the strongest men are moved to tears by his eloquence.

Easter Monday.

Good Friday was a pouring day, so that the ceremonies which usually take place in the open air, in the Piazza Grande, where a sepulchre had been prepared to receive the image of our Saviour's body, were restricted to the interior of the church of St. Michaele. When we went there at eight o'clock in the evening, we found the church crowded from end to end with people, who were chaunting the Miserere, and radiant with a thousand wax-lights, which sparkled in the huge glass chandeliers. In the choir, on a raised bier, under a catafalque of black cloth, and surrounded by a treble row of tall wax tapers, lay the body, for which the whole service was in fact a funeral ceremony. Soon after we arrived, a sudden hush in the crowd, shewed that something important was going to happen, and a huge friar's lanthorn carried in by a boy, was the predecessor of the " Pilgrim Father of the Riviera" himself. This celebrated Capuchin monk is now quite an old man, with a long white beard, but is still sent forth from his convent, during Lent, to exercise his wonderful gift of preaching in the towns on the coast. His sermon was short, but most graphic and striking. He began by describing a dreadful murder which people committed upon the person of their kindest friend and benefactor, with the horror it excited; and then pointing to the white corpse which lay before him amid the blazing candles, he declared that those around him had themselves committed the crime, and that the object of it was no other than their Saviour, whose image they saw there pale and bleeding before their eyes. He ended by snatching the crucifix from the support by his side, and holding it aloft to entreat the people to repent, by the sufferings which they there saw figured. As he concluded, the military filed into the church, and then, amidst rolling of drums and blowing of trumpets, which filled up all the intervals of the chaunting, the body was taken up by the black penitents, and carried three times round the church. The penitents preceded it in their black robes, with their black crosses and silver lanthorns. At its head, was the Host in its shining golden monstrance, followed by the priests, while the Mentonese nobles supported the funeral canopy. The procession occupied more than an hour, but the chaunting and martial music were so varied, that it was scarcely tedious. We remained in a small chapel near the choir, where the altar had been opened to disclose a most terrible pietà statue, which looked as if it had fallen down in all the contorted agonies of violent death. It was touching, though sad, to see the circles of people kneeling round it at intervals, and the little children who kissed its gashed side, and its feet streaming with blood.

Easter Sunday.

"He is risen." The words have been proclaimed in triumphal chaunts by the priests and the religious orders in St. Michaele. The news has been echoed by the chorus of thousands of voices; the pillars and the altars have thrown off their mourning attire, and are again dressed up in crimson. The terrible pietas have been shut up in cupboards, to stay there till the Holy Week of next year, and all the shops are filled with the same gaily-painted eggs, which the children are playing with in the streets. The Mentonese may eat and dance again, for " Poor old Lent is dead," say the peasants, "and bad luck go with her."

AN EXCURSION IN APRIL.

AFTER long wishing to turn the Bordighera point, which has bounded at once our horizon and our expeditions, we have at length done so. We waited so long for a fine day in this blowy April weather, that at last we could wait no longer, and set off whilst a strong breeze was blowing in towards the coast, and breaking the waves into sheets of foam upon the rocky shore. Most beautiful the sea looked as we turned the point of our ambitions, long streaks of pale green streaming in upon the dark purple expanse of water, where the light broke through the storm clouds. On the other side of the bay, rays of sunshine fell upon the rifts in the great brown mountains, monotonous in their outline compared to those at Mentone, but still beautiful, as they stand round about St. Remo, which rises from the sea in tiers of white houses, with a fine church crowning the hill on which they are built. There are palm trees here as at Bordighera, but not such fine ones, although this is the place whence came Bresca, the trading sea-captain, who gave an order to throw water upon the ropes which held up the famous obelisk in front of St. Peter's, in defiance of the order of Pope Sixtus V., that any one who spoke should pay the penalty with his life, and who thus saved the obelisk, and obtained as reward that his native place of St. Remo, should furnish the Easter palms to St. Peter for ever. Early every spring, the palm branches are tied up to their stems, in order to bleach them for this purpose, and from that time till the autumn their chief beauty is lost; but here and there a graceful stem, crowned with umbrella-like foliage, rears itself still untouched in the little square gardens, among the tall houses.

Nevertheless, what strikes strangers far more than the palm trees, is the number of monks in St. Remo. From every narrow window along the main road, you are almost sure, if you wait long enough, to see a brown cowled head poke itself out, and a pointed white beard throw a long shadow on the yellow sunlit wall. The churches and doorways perfectly swarm with monks, and groups of them are perpetually to be met with, and stumbled over, kneeling before shrines in the dark street corners.

Opposite our windows at the pleasant inn of La Palma, was the splendid old palace of the Boria family. This is really as fine as any palace that can be seen in Genoa, and has a court-yard and staircase which would do honour to the abode of a sovereign. Some way behind this is a piazza, which contains the two principal churches of the lower town, and in one corner, an audacious statue, not often met with even in Italy, of God the Father. Hence, steep, narrow, and filthy little streets, arched overhead, and crowded with dirty children, cats, dogs, and chickens below, lead to the top of the hill, where there is a fine open terrace, lined with cypresses, which commands a lovely view of the mountains and sea. Here is a church, containing some splendid twisted pillars of yellow marble, and a hospital for leprosy, which terrible disease still lingers round St. Remo. There were eighteen patients in the hospital when we visited it, all hopelessly incurable, either their limbs or their faces being gradually eaten away, so that with several, while you look upon one side of the face, and see it apparently in the bloom of health and youth, the other has already fallen away and ceased to exist. The disease is hereditary, having remained in certain families of this district, almost from time immemorial. The members of these families are prohibited from intermarrying with those of others, or indeed from marrying at all, unless it is believed that they are free from any seeds of the fatal inheritance. Sometimes the marriages, when sanctioned by magistrates and clergy, are contracted in safety, but often, after a year or two of wedded life, the terrible enemy appears again, and existence becomes a curse; thus the fearful legacy is handed down. The lepers at St. Remo, find in its admirable hospital every alleviation of their miseries, and are most kindly cared for by Sisters of Charity.

We had heard so much of the mountain sanctuary of St. Romano, that we set out to visit it the very evening of our arrival at St. Remo. A long stony way leads thither from the hospital, a most fatiguing walk, and a labour that scarcely repays one. Each turn made us desire more to be at the end of our fatigues, and each turn only disclosed a new stony ascent, longer and more tedious than the last; and at length, when we thought we were just arriving, the sanctuary came in sight, but on the furthest summit of a distant hill. However, we would not give in, and at last we reached it. A large white mitred statue of St. Romano, lies in a lower chapel with a sword through its breast, on the spot where the saint, who was bishop of Genoa, suffered martyrdom. This chapel is attached to and encloses the cave in which he lived in retirement. The upper chapel is dark, empty, and desolate, but stands in a wood of old gnarled chesnut trees, beneath which the mossy grass was enamelled with large blue gentians.

Early the following morning we set out for Taggia, in a queer carriage with two rope-harnessed horses, and the most hideous old man we ever saw in our lives for a driver. The road thither follows the highway for some distance, passing beneath the sanctuary of La Madonna della Guardia, on a high green hill rightly named the Capo Verde, and turning off near the village of La Riva, a row of houses on the shore, with an old ruined tower above them. Hence, it is a lovely drive through luxuriant olives, carpeted with green flax and corn, and surrounded by high mountains, on the steep sides of which, the town of Castellaro soon appears upon the right, and beyond it, the famous sanctuary of Lampedusa, jammed into a narrow ledge of the precipice.

Taggia itself is deep down in the valley by the side of the rushing river of the same name. Its streets are curious; many of the houses have once been grand palazzi, and there is still a native aristocracy resident in the place. Many of the old buildings are painted on the outside with fading frescoes, of others the stone fronts are cut into diamond facets, others are adorned with rich carving; most of them rest upon open arches, in which are shops, where umbrella vendors set out their bright wares, and crimson beretti hang out for sale, enlivening the grey walls by their brilliant colouring. As we got out of the carriage, a crowd gathered round us—"Did we wish to see the house of Dr. Antonio?" "Would we see the house in which il Baronetto Inglese had resided?" or, "Was it the house of the Signora Eleanora we wanted?" Thus Signor Ruffini, by his Doctor Antonio, has created local interests and associations for his native town, as Sir Walter

Scott has done for the banks of Loch Katrine and Loch Achray. The brother of Signor Ruffini still has a house at Taggia, and the author himself has frequently resided there. The house described as that of Signora Eleanora, is detached from the town, standing in an old-fashioned garden of its own. The native artist mentioned in the novel is now dead, having been cut off in the bloom of his life and genius, but some beautiful drawings from his works may be seen in the house of his brother, who kindly allows strangers to inspect them. The theatre where "Signor Orlando Pistacchini" performed before the Davennes, stands near the path leading to Castellaro, and is attached to the palace of the Marchesa. After exploring Taggia, with its narrow streets and old churches, whose pillars were still swathed in the red stockings by which the Italian Church shows her Easter rejoicings, we set out across the long narrow bridge which spans the valley, and bears witness to the frequent inundations of its obstreperous river. Midway upon the bridge stands a shrine with an image of the Madonna. This is a memorial of an earthquake, which in 1831 destroyed its third and eleventh arches. Two children, brother and sister, who were crossing at the very instant of the shock, were thrown down with this, the eleventh arch, and, wonderful to relate, sustained no injury; in acknowledgment of which miraculous escape, the grateful father erected the shrine, with an inscription to commemorate the story.

A path turning to the right at the end of the bridge soon mounts the hill by a steep ascent to Castellaro. Here we toiled up in the burning sun, with some peasants driving their heavily-laden donkeys before us, both they and we stopping from time to time to take breath, and to gather the beautiful flowers which grew by the way side. Castellaro when reached, turns out to be a long straggling village, without much feature; but the church, as seen from the road to Lampedusa, stands out finely upon the spur of the hill, its gaily-painted tower relieved against the blue background of sea.

"A broad, smooth road, opening from Castellaro northwards, and stretching over the side of the steep mountain in capricious zig-zags, now conceals, now gives to view the front of the sanctuary, shaded by two oaks of enormous dimensions. The Castellini, who made this road 'in the sweat of their brows,' point it out with pride, and well they may. They tell you with infinite complacency, how every one of the pebbles with which it is paved, was brought from the sea-shore, those who had mules using them for that purpose, those who had none bringing up loads on their own backs; how every one, gentleman and peasant, young and old, women and boys, worked day and night, with no other inducement than the love of the Madonna. The Madonna of Lampedusa is their creed, their occupation, their pride, their *carroccio*, their fixed idea.

"All that relates to the miraculous image, and the date and mode of its translation to Castellaro, is given at full length in two inscriptions, one in Latin, the other in bad Italian verses, which are to be seen in the interior of the little chapel of the sanctuary. Andrea Anfosso, a native of Castellaro, being the captain of a privateer, was one day attacked and defeated by the Turks, and carried to the Isle of Lampedusa. Here he succeeded in making his escape, and hiding himself until the Turkish vessel which had captured his left the island. Anfosso, being a man of expedients, set about building a boat, and finding himself in a great dilemma what to do for a sail, ventured on the bold and original step of taking from the altar of some church or chapel of the island, a picture of the Madonna to serve as one; and so well did it answer his purpose, that he made a most prosperous voyage back to his native shores, and, in a fit of generosity, offered his holy sail to the worship of his fellow-townsmen. The wonder of the affair does not stop here. A place was chosen by universal acclamation, two gun-shots in advance of the present sanctuary, and a chapel erected, in which the gift was deposited with all due honour. But the Madonna, as it would seem, had an insurmountable objection to the spot selected, for, every morning that God made, the picture was found at the exact place where the actual church now stands. Sentinels were posted at the door of the chapel, the entire village remained on foot for nights, mounting guard at the entrance—no precaution, however, availed. In spite of the strictest watch, the picture, now undeniably a miraculous one, found means to make its way to the spot it preferred. At length, the Castellari came to understand that it was the Madonna's express will, that her headquarters should be shifted to where her resemblance betook itself every night, and though it had pleased her to make choice of the most abrupt and the steepest spot on the whole mountain, just where it was requisite to raise arches in order to lay a sure foundation for her sanctuary, the Castellini set themselves *con amore* to the task so clearly revealed to them, and this widely-renowned chapel was completed. This took place in 1619. In the course of time some rooms were annexed, for the accommodation of visitors and pilgrims, and a terrace built, and many other additions and embellishments are even now in contemplation, and no doubt will be accomplished some day; for, although the Castellini have but a small purse, their's is the great lever which can remove all impediments—the faith that brought about the Crusades.

"To the north a long, long vista of deep, dark, frowning gorges, closes in the distance by a gigantic screen of snow-clad Alps—the glorious expanse of the Mediterranean to the south—east and west, range upon range of gently undulating hills, softly inclining towards the sea—in the plain below, the fresh, cozy valley of Taggia, with its sparkling track of waters, and rich belt of gardens, looking like a perfect mosaic of every gradation of green, chequered with winding silver arabesques. Ever and anon a tardy pomegranate in full blossom spreads out its oriflamme of tulip-shaped dazzling red flowers. From the rising ground opposite frowns mediæval Taggia, like a discontented guest at a splendid banquet. A little further off westward, the eye takes in the Campanile of the Dominican Church, emerging from a group of cypresses, and further still, on the extreme verge of the western cliff, the sanctuary of our lady of the Guardia, shows its white silhouette against the dark blue sky."

On our return to St. Remo, we decided to go on from thence as far as our finances would allow, and finding early on the following morning, that a little omnibus was going to start for Porto Maurizio, we determined to take advantage of it to help us thus far on our way. So having obtained places in the Coupé for two francs apiece, and bargained that the vehicle should wait a few minutes while we put up our things; we were soon leaving St. Remo far behind, three brisk little horses galloping before us, their bells ringing merrily through the fresh dew-laden olive woods. We passed through St. Stefano al Mare which contains nothing remarkable, and St. Lorenzo al Mare with a peculiar church tower, standing close against the sea, in tiers of varied gradation, and then Porto Maurizio came in sight rising from the water in rows of handsome houses which cover the steep sides of its promontory.

The wind was bitterly sharp as we emerged into the wretched street, and its furious blasts whistled through the crypt-like entrance of the inn. We were so cold, that it looked as if there was even less to see than there was, all was so dead and white, cut out sharply against the sky. The church especially, though handsome, was new and perfectly white, which was dull by comparison with the other gaily-painted churches of the Riviera. So, much disappointed in Porto Maurizio, we made our way back to the inn and bargaining for a carriage to take us at diligence price, engaged it for fifteen francs to Albenga, where we arrived long before dark, in time to wander about the curious old town, and to count its extraordinary towers, which rise out of the plain like a number of tall ninepins set close together. Albenga affords many subjects well worth drawing, and to the architect it is a perfect treasure city, possessing a very ancient gothic cathedral, an early christian Baptistery all green with mould and damp, and three equally grim and green Lombardic lions, besides all the before-mentioned towers, which are sprinkled about among the houses in the most profuse and apparently purposeless manner. The view from the entrance of the town is quite lovely, for it is situated in a valley so fruitful and fertile that it looks like one great garden, lying between undulating hills, and closed in at the end by a range of fine snow mountains which rise up like ghosts in the yellow sunset. It required all the charms of Albenga, however, to make us think its inn (Albergo d'Italia) supportable, our ill-paved bedrooms were so stuffy and dirty, and so little food was to be obtained. The people too were not over anxious to take us in at all, "No travellers ever wanted to sleep at Albenga," they said. Nevertheless, on our persuading them at last that we were an exception and could not think of going any further, they gave us lodging, with coarse pasta, boiled in oil, and some horribly tough cutlets for dinner.

Rumour, Murray, and the desire of seeing things which other people generally leave unseen, alike made us long to visit Garlanda, and we pressed the only carriage which Albenga afforded into service for the purpose, a kind of open tabernacle on wheels, like a huge litter of ancient times, of which we obtained possession for the day for eight francs.

It is a lovely drive up the green Albenga valley. Overhead are tall peach trees, which, when we saw them, were bursting into a luxuriance of pink blossom. Beneath these the vines cling in Bacchanalian festoons, leaping from tree to tree, and below all, large melons, young corn, and bright green flax, waving here and there into sheets of blue flowers, form the carpet of nature. Sometimes gaily-painted towers, and ancient palazzi, with carved armorial gateways, and arched porticoes break in upon the solitude of the valley. In one of these, the palace of Lusignano, which is girt about on two sides by the steep escarpment of the mountains, and backed by a noble pine tree, Madame de Genlis lived for some time, considering her abode an arcadia. A curious relic of ancient times, which must have been one of the principal objects in the view from her windows, is a gigantic naked stone figure sitting astride upon the wall, close to her garden gate. A short distance beyond this, the road runs by the side of the clear rushing Centa, to whose crystal waters the plain is indebted for its luxuriance. Here the mountains form rugged precipices towards the river, only leaving a space for the road to pass between. A little further on, the river itself divides to embrace the mediæval walls and towers of Villa-Nuova, a curious and tiny city. Near the road is a round church, which with a gothic tower adjoining it, built of deep yellow stone, forms a picturesque subject for the artist.

Hence, across the marshy plain of the Lerone, which was one sheet of brilliant spring flowers, we arrived at an old chateau, with Scotch-looking pepper box tourelles, which guards the narrowing fastness of the valley. This is the castle of Garlanda, and beyond it is the church, around which the peasantry of the valley gathered in defence of their beloved Domenichino, when an attempt was lately made to remove it. This famous picture, which is covered by a curtain, hangs near the entrance. It is certainly one of the loveliest of the works of its great painter (1581-1641). Kugler says of him, that "he seldom succeeded in the higher subjects of inspiration," and so it is here; the Virgin is only a lovely but simple country girl, holding a beautiful curly-headed child; St. Mauro is a handsome young man kneeling before her, but there is a truthfulness about each figure which makes them difficult to forget. The other remarkable picture in the church, the martyrdom of St. Erasmus, by Poussin, is almost too horrible to look at. The young curé of the village who fills the office of school master and sacristan, shewed us the pictures himself. He told us how he had been born and bred in the place, and how rejoiced he was to be permitted while so young to come back and minister to the people he knew so well. When we had seen the relics, we found ourselves almost fainting with hunger, but contrived to capture a cow, of whose milk we drank under the shade of the olives, with some bread and figs. As we returned, we sent home our carriage from Villa-Nuova, and walked back through the rocky lanes fringed with yellow genista, not arriving at Albenga till sunset, when all the bells in the red towers were ringing the merriest Ave-Maria imaginable, and the whole plain was bathed in gold.

The old man who drove us to Garlanda was so anxious to take us on to Savona, that on his consenting to go for fifteen francs, we agreed to employ him. The drive was very amusing, but less beautiful than we had expected. We stopped in the market-place of Pietra to see the carvings in the church, which, though mentioned by Murray, are not very remarkable. Then we drew for two hours on the beach at Finale, while the horses rested, and visited a splendidly-attired Madonna, with real hair, standing in a golden artificial light in the church. The rocks beyond Finale are very grand, and the descent to the sea shore, flanked by their gigantic precipices, on one of which is a tall mediæval tower, is certainly the finest scene on this part of the coast.

At two p.m. the long line of white houses which form the town of Savona came in sight, and at three we entered the streets, and descended at the excellent Hotel Suisse. We immediately hired a little carriage for six francs, in the piazza, to go to the Santuario. It was a quaint little charrette in which we were jolted up and down to such a degree, that it was a difficult matter to keep our seats at all. The drive was lovely, through a mountain ravine and by a rushing torrent, which three years ago overflowed its banks and carried away houses, bridges and people, everything on its course, so that the road was still very bad. After many windings of the valley we entered a courtyard, shaded by huge elm trees, just bursting into their first green; in the centre was a fountain splashing with white foam, and at the further end a fine church, which contains a presentation of the Virgin by Domenichino, and some good pictures by Bernardo Castello. The story of the miraculous Virgin in honour of whom the sanctuary was founded, was formerly sold in a thick volume, but it is now out of print, and does not seem likely to be republished. Her first appearance is said to have taken place at the little round chapel on the hill above the present sanctuary, where she showed herself to a poor countryman, and desired him to go into Savona, and declare what he had seen. This he did boldly, and was put into prison for his pains, but an unknown lady came to open his prison doors and release him. Again at the scene of his daily labours, the Virgin revealed herself to him, and again desired him to go and tell what he had seen in Savona, but he remonstrated, saying that the last time she had told him to do this he had obeyed her, and had been imprisoned in consequence. "Yes," answered the Virgin, "and it was I who released you; go then again boldly, and I will protect you." So he obeyed, and went to tell what he had seen in Savona, but the people mocked and no one believed him, and he returned home sorrowful. On his way as he was pondering sadly over these things, he met a great multitude of people: " Whence do you come," he said, " and what are you going to do." " Oh," they said, " we are the inhabitants of the Albergo dei Poveri, and we are going to Savona, that we may obtain food and continue to live, for we have no corn left in our granaries." Then he bade them return for their granaries should be filled. And they were unbelieving, yet still they returned, and when they reached the granaries, they were unable to open the door on account of the quantity of grain that was in them. All the people of Savona when they saw the miracle, gave praise to the Virgin who had delivered them; and now, convinced of the truth of the countryman's story, they built the famous church and hospital in her honour, which are still to be seen in the valley of St. Bernardo.

Within, the church is perfectly magnificent, its walls

being entirely covered with precious marbles, which in their turn are encrusted with the votive offerings of gold and silver; these, with the splendid golden chandeliers swinging from the roof, make a mass of colouring which would be quite dazzling were it not subdued by the thickness of the masonry, and the natural darkness of the arched recesses. The under church is even more splendid than the upper, its walls being one mass of precious stones and metal. Here is the famous image of the Virgin, hideously radiant in the jewelled crown of Pope Pius VII, and the diamond collar of King Charles Albert. Beside her kneels a little marble figure of the countryman to whom her discovery was due. Beneath her feet issues a stream of water, served to visitors from a massive silver jug upon a silver tray; "holy water," the sacristan said, "and competent to cure all manner of diseases," but we did not find it so, for it was so icy cold, that we were ill all the evening after drinking it. The music at the Santuario was quite beautiful. On the Saturday afternoon that we were there, the Litany was most sweetly sung by the inmates of the neighbouring poor-house and orphanage, all looking most picturesque; the younger women in white veils (pezzottos), the elder wearing over their heads scarfs with brightly-coloured flowers (mezzaras). When the service was over, they emerged from the church in a long regular procession, two and two, with crosses carried before them.

We had not much time on our return left for Savona, and the house and tomb of Chiabrera were rather imagined than seen. Nevertheless we visited the cathedral, and very fine it looked in the flickering lamplight which fell in fitful gleams over the groups of sculptured figures which still stood in the aisle, where they had borne a part in the ceremonies of Passion week and Easter—" figures quite worth their weight in gold," a worshipper stopped his devotions to tell us, and that must have been a great deal, for they were perfect colossi.

We did not wish to spend our Sunday, even in beautiful Savona, and so engaged a little carriage to take us to Voltri, and started at half-past three in the dark morning, to catch the early train to Genoa. It was a drive of four hours, but the early morning was lovely, and the hills and the distant light-house of Genoa, were crimson in the new-born sunshine. Half-an-hour's rail brought us from Voltri to Genoa, and *what* a view it is which you have on entering the town, truly "La Superba," rising in tier above tier of palaces and churches, from the still deep blue waters of the harbour crowded with shipping. By eight o'clock we were safely established in comfortable rooms in the excellent Hotel de la Ville, looking down on the busy port, and on the quays, crowded with gay young soldiers and women in flowing white veils. After the English service, which is held in two rooms in the handsome newly-built Via Assarotti, we went to the promenade of the Acqua Sole, which was all lovely spring and sunshine, trees bursting into leaf and flower, fountains splashing, the sea gleaming in the distance, and numbers of well-dressed towns people and handsome young officers in brilliant new uniforms walking about. The beauty of the inhabitants of Genoa surprised us more at every turn, and I believe all strangers are equally struck with it.

From Acqua Sole we went into the town to see the Lombard cloister of St. Stefano, which is very curious and interesting, and then into some of the narrower and older streets. Every part of the town abounds in historical relics, old doorways over which are sculptures representing either some event of the family history within, or some event of the family history within, or some legend of its patron saint; old deserted monasteries with decaying courtyards, old street corners rich with faded pictures and carvings. Almost all the houses deserve looking at where the streets are wide enough for you to see them. "In the smaller streets the wonderful novelty of everything, the unusual smells, the unaccountable filth (though Genoa is reckoned the cleanest of Italian towns), the disorderly jumbling of dirty houses, one upon the roof of another; the passages more squalid and more close than any in St. Giles's, or in old Paris; in and out of which, not vagabonds, but well-dressed women, with white veils and great fans, were passing and repassing; the entire absence of any resemblance in any dwelling-house, or shop, or wall, or post, or pillar, to anything one has ever seen before; and the disheartening dirt, discomfort and decay, perfectly confound one. One is only conscious of a feverish and bewildered vision of saints, and virgin's shrines at the street corners; of great numbers of friars, monks, and soldiers; of vast red curtains waving at the doorways of churches; of always going up-hill, and yet seeing every other street and passage going higher up; of fruit stalls, with fresh lemons and oranges hanging in garlands made of vine-leaves."—"And the majority of the streets are as narrow as any thoroughfare can well be, where people (even Italian people) are supposed to live and walk about, being mere lanes, with here and there a kind of well, or breathing place. The houses are immensely high, painted in all sorts of colours, and are in every stage and state of damage, dirt, and lack of repair. They are commonly let off in floors or flats, like the houses in the old town of Edinburgh, or many houses in Paris. There are few street doors; the entrance halls are, for the most part, looked upon as public property; and any moderately enterprising scavenger might make a fine fortune by now and then cleaning them out.

"But when can one forget the streets of palaces; the Strada Nuova and the Strada Balbi; or how the former looks when seen under the brightest and most intensely blue of summer skies; which its narrow perspective of immense mansions reduces to a tapering and most precious strip of brightness, looking down upon the heavy shade below. The endless details of these rich palaces; the walls of some of them within, alive with masterpieces, of Vandyke. The great heavy stone balconies one above another, and tier above tier, with here and there one larger than the rest, towering high up—a huge marble platform; the doorless vestibules, massively-barred lower windows, immense public staircases, thick marble pillars, strong, dungeon-like arches, and dreary, dreaming, echoing, vaulted chambers, among which the eye wanders again, and again, and again, as every palace is succeeded by another; the terrace gardens between house and house, with green arches of the vine, and groves of orange trees, and blushing oleanders in full bloom, twenty, thirty, forty feet above the street; the painted halls mouldering and blotting and rotting in the damp corners, and still shining out in bright colours and voluptuous designs where the walls are dry; the faded figures on the outsides of the houses, holding wreaths, and crowns, and flying upward and downward, and standing in niches, and here and there looking fainter and more feeble than elsewhere by contrast with some fresh little cupids, who on a more recently decorated portion of the front, are stretching out what seems to be the semblance of a blanket, but is, indeed, a sun-dial; the steep, steep, uphill streets of small palaces (but very large palaces for all that) with marble terraces looking down into close by-ways, the magnificent and innumerable churches; and the rapid passage from a street of stately edifices into a maze of the vilest squalor, steaming with unwholesome stenches, and swarming with half-naked children, and whole worlds of dirty people, make up, altogether, such a scene of wonder; so lively and yet so dead; so noisy and yet so quiet; so obtrusive and yet so shy and lowering; so wide awake and yet so fast asleep; that it is a sort of intoxication to a stranger to walk on, and on, and on, and look about him. A bewildering phantasmagoria, with all the inconsistency of a dream, and all the pain and all the pleasure of an extravagant reality."

Thus Dickens admirably describes Genoa in his most pictorial "Pictures of Italy," and thus every stranger sees it and feels it.

One of the most interesting spots in the town is the Piazza St. Matteo, in the heart of the city, on a straight line with the cathedral. This was formerly called the Piazza Doria, and is consecrated by the relics of that great family. Its ancient church of striped black and white marble contains their tombs; in its very remarkable cloisters are the remains of the statues presented to Andrea Doria by the Republic, while a palace of the same character as the church, bears the inscription,—" S. C. Andreæ de Auria Patria Liberatori Munus Publicum."

> "This house was Andrea Doria's. Here he lived;
> And here at eve relaxing, when ashore,
> Held many a pleasant, many a grave discourse
> With them that sought him, walking to and fro
> As on his deck. 'Tis less in length and breadth
> Than many a cabin in a ship of war;
> But 'tis of marble, and at once inspires
> The reverence due to ancient dignity.

> He left it for a better, and 'tis now
> A house of trade, the meanest merchandize
> Cumbering its floors. Yet, fallen as it is,
> 'Tis still the noblest dwelling—even in Genoa!
> And hadst thou, Andrea, lived there to the last,
> Thou hadst done well; for there is that without,
> That in the wall which monarchs could not give,
> Nor thou take with thee, that which says aloud,
> It was thy Country's gift to her Deliverer.
>
> 'Tis in the heart of Genoa (he who comes,
> Must come on foot) and in a place of stir;
> Men on their daily business, early and late,
> Thronging thy very threshold. But when there,
> Thou wert among thy fellow-citizens,
> Thy children, for they hail thee as their sire;
> And on a spot thou must have loved, for there,
> Calling them round, thou gav'st them more than life,
> Giving what, lost, makes life not worth the keeping.
> There thou did'st do indeed, an act divine;
> Nor could'st thou leave thy door or enter in,
> Without a blessing on thee."
>
> *Rogers.*

The best views of Genoa which are easy of access, are to be obtained from the Scoglietto gardens beyond the Doria Palace, which consist of a series of terraces planted with an abundance of camphor, pepper, and other curious trees, mingled with beautiful flowers, or from the terrace of the Sauli church, on the other side of the town. This church is approached by the Ponte di Carignano, built by the great family of that name, who, while rivalling the Saulis in greatness of present wealth and popularity, desired to rival them also in the greatness they left behind for posterity to gaze upon. Both works are magnificent, but the church especially is remarkable as that of one private family, of which a daughter is the only representative now remaining. It contains some gigantic statues by Puget and David, and in its sacristy a lovely picture by Albert Durer of St. Fabian and St. Augustin.

A charming expedition may be made from Genoa to the promontory of Porto Fino, which it takes two days to explore thoroughly. This excursion gives a very good idea of the scenery of the Riviera di Levante, of which it is perhaps one of the most favorable specimens. In the richer and more varied vegetation of its vallies, and in its turfy instead of rocky mountains, it is perhaps more strictly beautiful, though less picturesque, than the Riviera di Ponente. We took a carriage as far as Camoglia, following the high road to Sarzana as far as Recco, and passing through Albaro (where there is a picturesque ruined church upon the sea-shore), Quarto, Quinto, and Nervi. In one of these villages is a curious specimen of Italian wall-painting as illustrative of the lives of those within. A happy marriage, the subsequent elopement of the bride, and its miserable consequences, are all pourtrayed upon the walls, each figure being an actual portrait and as large as life. They were placed there by the husband, who avenged himself on his faithless wife by thus exposing her, she herself being obliged to pass the house door whenever she drives into Genoa from her neighbouring villa. Nervi has a lovely view of the promontory and rocks of Porto Fino, and exquisite gardens reaching down to the sea-shore, but it must be dull as a winter residence from being so shut in by the hills which rise abruptly behind the town, there being literally no *space* for walks except those along the highroad. The " stabilimento Inglese " is however a large and comfortable lodging-house, and is let in a series of small apartments, whose inmates may either live en Pension, or keep entirely to themselves.

"Camoglia seen from the road above, is like a tiny model on the margin of the dimpled water, shining in the sun. Descended into, by the winding mule-tracks, it is a perfect miniature of a primitive sea-faring town; the saltest, roughest, most piratical little place that ever was seen. Great rusty iron rings and mooring chains, capstans, and fragments of old masts and spars, choke up the way; hardy rough weather boats, and seamen's clothing, flutter in the little harbour, or are drawn out on the sunny stones to dry; on the parapet of the rude pier, a few amphibious-looking fellows lie asleep, with their legs dangling over the wall, as though earth or water were all one to them; and if they slipped in, they would float away, dozing comfortably among the fishes; the church is bright with trophies of the sea, and votive offerings in commemoration of some escape from storm and shipwreck. The dwellings not immediately abutting on the harbour, are approached by blind low archways, and by crooked steps, as if, in darkness and in difficulty of access, they should be like holds of ships, or inconvenient cabins under water; and everywhere there is a smell of fish, and sea-weed, and old rope."—*Dickens.*

Behind the town rise on a hill, the grounds of an old villa, overgrown with a wild luxuriance of cypress, oak, ilex, myrtle, and laburnam, which in April strews the ground with its golden flowers. At the top are some pine trees, whence on one side you look down over precipitous cliffs to the sea, and on the other through the woods to the village of Ruta, embedded on the green mountain side. We wandered on from thence to a ruined chapel near the seashore, but it is not much worth seeing, and the walk from thence to Ruta is so hot and fatiguing, we cannot recommend others to follow our example. The wild flowers on these mountain sides are quite beautiful, including endless varities of orchis, primulas, gentians, and hepaticas.

Ruta, which possesses two very good though primitive inns, is situated almost on the edge of the mountain ridge, which as it runs out further into the sea, forms the peninsula of Porto Fino. Close to the upper inn, is the mouth of the short tunnel, on passing through which you first really enter the sunny gardens of the south, and whence you look over a swelling luxuriance of peaches and almonds, carpeted with melons, and garlanded with vines, to Rapallo, Chiavari and Sestri, lying in brilliant whiteness by the side of the deep blue water, and thence to the mountains, at whose point the coral rocks of Porto Venere, form the entrance of the lovely gulf of Spezia. The view towards Genoa also was most striking in the sunset, mountains and city and lighthouse and sea, alike bathed with crimson as the sun went down behind the horizon of waters.

At five o'clock the next morning we set out to walk along the rocky ledge above the tunnel, in order to descend into the woods, before the sun had attained its power. Deep down below we saw the convent of San Fruttuoso, lying among its palm trees in a cleft, by the sea-shore, the place where the Dorias are now brought by sea for burial, and where their strange sarcophagus tombs may be seen in the crypt. This spot had a melancholy interest some years ago, from the burning of a fine ship which had only left Genoa a few hours before. Two heroic peasant women put off in a small boat to save the crew, and one of them was lost in the attempt. Porto Fino is an interesting and curious little town, (about three miles from Ruta,) situated in a tiny bay near the point of the promontory. The houses are supported by open arcades, the church is gaily painted, a fine umbrella pine tree shades the neighbouring rocks, and the harbour is crowded with picturesque fishing boats. All the men in the town are fishermen, with tall red beretti on their heads, and the women are lace makers, who sit at their pillows all day under the shady arcades beneath the houses. An enchanting terrace-walk of a mile, through the ilex woods overhanging the sea, leads round the point of the bay from Porto Fino, to the little cove of Piccolo Paggi, where a yellow castle on a rock forms a picturesque foreground to the purple mountains. There we dined beside a little fern-fringed fountain, and then went on in a boat (which followed us from the harbour) to Santa Margherita, about half-an-hour's row distant. Perhaps the finest point in the whole promontory is seen by going this way; the convent of Cervaro or Sylvano, now a ruin, on a rock surrounded by gigantic palm trees and aloes, which is the place where Francis the first was confined before he was conveyed to Catalonia. Unfortunately, an English nobleman, lately resident at Nervi, has so raised the prices of everything in this neighbourhood, by his lavish expenditure, that it is very necessary to come to an agreement with your boatmen before leaving Porto Fino, as the gratuities, which three years ago were received with the utmost gratitude, are now rejected with scorn, and even violence.

Santa Margherita is a picturesque little town, and a worthy ending to so beautiful an excursion. Here we found our carriage waiting for us, and returned to Genoa, in time to have tea beneath the orange trees, in the brilliantly lighted Café della Concordia, before it was closed for the night.

We had still three days left, so we determined to make a tourette into Lombardy, which the railway now renders very easy from Genoa. So after a day spent in flying across the green corn plains, with fresh young vines twining beneath the mulberry trees, we came in sight of Piacenza, in the sunset, in time to walk along the ramparts, fringed with brown convents and churches, and to look down towards the purple Apennines, and the infant Po, now a blue rivulet, flowing through a wide stony bed, which it fills in winter. The piazza of Piacenza is one of the most striking in Italy; on one side is the Saracenic-looking town-hall, of a deep orange colour, in front of which stand the great bronze statues of the Farneses; on the other, down a long street of overhanging houses, is seen the cathedral, with an arched front, projecting porches resting on red granite lions, and a tall tower, with the iron cage still hanging to it, in which the Farneses exposed their state criminals.

The following day we saw the old church of St. Donino, remarkable for its quaint carvings and extraordinarily hideous monsters, and went on in the evening to Parma, a dreary deserted looking town, in which the wide streets seem only peopled by the flocks of pigeons which come swooping down from their holes in the old houses. The cathedral is full of dim quaint frescoes of Coreggio, in which nobody can see anything but a chaos of arms and legs, and the churches have other frescoes, which are blacker and more undistinguishable still. Beside the cathedral rises the baptistery, with tiers of square arches in red marble. The great rambling palace is chiefly a shrine for the paintings of Coreggio, but it possesses also the ruined theatre of the Farneses, "one of the dreariest spectacles of decay that ever was seen."

Modena, to which we went for a few hours from Parma, we thought even less interesting—nothing to be seen but the cathedral with its quaint monsters, and the palace with its picture gallery, and all the lovely objects belonging to the Duke, which the people have confiscated, instead of his having, as the newspapers represented at the time, carried off *all their* pictures; the fact being, that he saved only one out of all his treasures, a " Piccola Madonna di Raffaello," which he carried off under his cloak.

Reggio, where we stayed for a few hours, is a very dull town, but has a fine view from the ramparts, of the Apennines around the ruined walls of Canossa, celebrated from the severity of Hildebrand, and the penance of the emperor Henry the fourth.

From Parma we came rapidly back to Mentone. Leaving at eleven p.m., we arrived at Genoa at half-past nine, and at Voltri at half-past eleven a.m. Hence we persuaded a driver of a small carriage to take us on to Savona for nine francs, and another again to take us from Savona to Oneglia for twenty-five. Travelling through the night, by the moonlit sea, and sometimes leaving our horses to rest for an hour, and walking before them along the shore, we reached Oneglia at three a.m., and there taking the diligence, arrived at Mentone before eleven.

For the benefit of future travellers, it may be mentioned, that the expense of the whole journey, during thirteen days, for three persons, was about fifteen pounds.

FAREWELLS.

May.

THESE were the last days at Mentone for which we came back, and they would have been very melancholy, if we could ever have realized that we were going away, before the time came. But, for so many months the rest of the world had been shut out, and our interests and pleasures had been so concentrated in the place we were in, that we had almost forgotten the outside world, and the necessity for returning to it.

In our last expedition to Ventimiglia, we did not drive as far as the town, but left the carriage at the entrance of a rocky path to the left, a little beyond the village of St. Agostino, and scrambled up the hills from thence, through the wild thyme and rosemary, for a distance of about a mile-and-a-half, to where the Claudian castle with its mouldering towers, stands on the highest spur of the yellow tufa rock. All around is a chaos of broken mountains: it is an utter solitude, and the scenery is wild in the highest degree. A rugged path leads down from the castle to the gate of the town near the Romanesque church.

Our last ride at Mentone was with Theresine Ravellina, through the pine woods to the little chapel of Santa Lucia. That mountain path had never looked so lovely, the sea seen through the trees was of the deepest blue, and nightingales sang in all the thick parts of the wood, which were carpeted with genista and heath, mingled with lilies and amaranthes, and all the orchideous flowers of May.

Then came the last day, and the farewells, with showers of bouquets from every one, rich and poor. Theresine, with little Pauline her daughter, brought immense ones, which they bestowed upon us, with declarations that they should pray on every fête day that they might see us again, though they did not suppose they ever should. "Mais," added Theresine as usual, "si le bon Dieu le veut, il ne faut pas se facher."

www.ingramcontent.com/pod-product-compliance
Lightning Source LLC
Chambersburg PA
CBHW021939240426
43669CB00047B/554